浙江省"十一五"重点教材建设项目

Spoken English for International Business

商务英语口语

主　编　曹深艳

副主编　王慧盛　张　帆

编　委　张万里　刘东光　张　敏　于　洋
　　　　王娟萍　郭　颖　申德安

北京大学出版社
PEKING UNIVERSITY PRESS

图书在版编目(CIP)数据

商务英语口语/曹深艳主编. —北京：北京大学出版社，2011.1
（21 世纪商务英语系列教材）
ISBN 978-7-301-18388-5

I. ①商…　II. ①曹…　III. ①商务－英语－口语－高等学校：技术学校－教材　IV. ①H319.9

中国版本图书馆 CIP 数据核字（2011）第 001784 号

书　　　　名：**商务英语口语**
著作责任者：曹深艳　主编
责　任　编　辑：叶　丹
标　准　书　号：ISBN 978-7-301-18388-5/H · 2737
出　版　发　行：北京大学出版社
地　　　　址：北京市海淀区成府路 205 号　100871
网　　　　址：http://www.pup.cn
电　子　信　箱：zbing@pup.pku.edu.cn
电　　　　话：邮购部 62752015　发行部 62750672　编辑部 62754382　出版部 62754962
印　　刷　　者：北京大学印刷厂
经　　销　　者：新华书店
　　　　　　　787 毫米×1092 毫米　16 开本　7 印张　188 千字
　　　　　　　2011 年 1 月第 1 版　2018 年 1 月第 4 次印刷
定　　　　价：19.00 元

前　言

本教材编写以突出高职特点，培养学生岗位适应能力为宗旨，注重教材的职业性、实践性、针对性、趣味性和实用性。

职业性

教材内容的选取以工作任务为主线，15个教学任务均与外贸公司等外向型企业中的外贸业务员、商务助理等职业岗位工作任务相对应，内容涵盖此类职业岗位所必需的金融、外贸、涉外接待等方面的基本业务知识与技巧，培养学生使用英语进行工作的能力，使学生在完成课程的学习之后就能适应基本工作要求，处理简单工作任务。

实践性

教学内容的组织以培养学生实践操作能力为重心，紧密联系工作实际，以解决工作任务为线索，进行实践教学设计。减少单纯理论讲解，增加"学做合一"项目设计，鼓励学生动口动手。同时，业内人士实战经验的设计使课堂更贴近社会、贴近实践。

针对性

教材的编写针对高职教育培养定位，针对高职学生的学习实际以及高职学生的学习需要，不过高要求，不面面俱到，降低难度，减少理论讲解，控制篇幅，满足基本岗位工作要求，培养学生基本商务英语口语交际能力。

趣味性

每个单元均以相关视频资料欣赏导入，并以插图、知识与技巧的讨论和卡拉OK式的配音等手段，丰富课堂教学方法。而业内人士实战经验不仅提高了教学的实用性，也大大提高了学生的学习兴趣。

实用性

构建包括学生用书和超大容量教学配套资料包（学生MP3、教师教学资料及教学课件等）的立体化教材。学生用书和教师教学资料主要为课堂教学服务，学生MP3为学生课外模仿练习提供音频资料。教学资料丰富，有利于学生课堂内外的学习，方便教师开展个性化教学。

本教材定位明确，适用于高职高专国际贸易、国际商务、商务英语、涉外文秘和旅游管理等专业学生使用，还可以供商务人士学习参考。

　　本教材在行业专家和高职教育专家的指导下，由浙江金融职业学院国际商务系商务英语专业、国际商务专业和国际贸易专业教师共同编写完成。由于编写人员相关专业知识水平有限，书中难免有疏漏及不妥之处，我们真诚地希望得到行业专家、教师及其他读者的批评指正。

　　本书在编写过程中参考了大量的相关书籍，选用了福步外贸论坛（FOB Business Forum）部分资料，得到浙江工商大学刘法公教授、浙江金融职业学院方华研究员和张海燕副教授的指导，也得到北京大学出版社的支持，在此一并表示感谢。

编写组

2010年8月 于杭州

使 用 说 明

　　高职高专《商务英语口语》开课时间建议为一个学期（第五学期），共18周，每周2课时，共计36课时。其中，15个教学任务分30课时组织教学，测验2课时，机动4课时。

　　每个项目教学安排建议2个课时（90分钟），教学编排结构如下：

一、Learning Objective 明确学习目标，指导学生记录学习效果

　　每项任务首页设计包括本次学习的主要内容和效果记录，鼓励学生学习思考和总结。

二、Section A　Movie Time 看电影学口语（10分钟）

　　A. 电影故事情节简介

　　B. 电影片段欣赏

　　C. 中英对白欣赏

　　通过视频欣赏导入，轻松进入课堂学习任务。

三、Section B　Work and Learn 做中学（65分钟）

　　A. Business Communication Skills 和 Work Skills 两部分以学生自学为主

　　　1. 要求学生预习，并以个人或小组为单位，根据此部分内容进行情境表演。

　　　2. 教师点评，对学生表演中反映出的问题，进行讲解和纠正。

　　B. Words and Expressions 常用表达法介绍

　　C. Useful Sentence Patterns 常用句型介绍

　　D. Sample Dialogue 对话范例欣赏

　　E. Learn to Work 学中做

　　要求学生运用学过的知识和技巧，进行实践操作。

　　　1. 常用表达法操练

　　　2. 句型操练

　　　3. 配音练习

　　　　（分角色标准美音朗读，方便教师组织课堂配音练习、学生课后自主练习）

四、Section C　Lessons from the Professionals 业内人士经验谈（15分钟）

　　提供业内人士发表的经验教训，鼓励学生讨论。文中有值得借鉴的经验，也会有错误的认识，鼓励学生自主阅读并发现文中好的经验，汲取教训。不要求学生英语纠错，主要

就外贸操作等方面进行纠错讨论，并允许学生在表达困难时使用母语辅助表述。 此部分有两个特点：其一，为学生提供业内人士实战经验，真实、生动、实用。其二，其中有一些语言表达错误，但是基本不影响理解。教师可以借助此材料，鼓励学生大胆使用英语，增强信心。

书中主要人物介绍

1. Young Gang, general manager of K&S Group 杨刚，K&S集团总经理

2. Ding Na, sales manager of K&S Group 丁娜，K&S集团销售部经理

3. Lydia Wang, Ding Na's assistant 王莉迪，丁娜的助理

4. Li Lin, office secretary of K&S Group 李林，办公室秘书

5. Eddie Collins, purchasing manager of Malaysia Maiya Group 艾迪·柯林斯，马来西亚美亚公司采购部经理

6. Ying Qiang, sales manager of China Textiles Import and Export Co.Ltd. 英强，中国纺织品进出口公司销售部经理

7. Ella Black, import manager of American Hunters Company 艾拉·布莱克，美国汉特公司进口部经理

目　录

Task One   At the Trade Fair

任务一 展会接待

Learning Objective

Be able to talk freely with a visitor to your booth at the trade fair.
Be able to talk briefly and effectively about your products.

My Gains

Business etiquette	
Work skills	
Language skills	

My Problems

Business etiquette	
Work skills	
Language skills	

Section A
Movie Time

Watch the video clip and answer the question.

What do you know about the Canton Fair?

Welcome to the 105th Canton Fair (China's No.1 Fair)

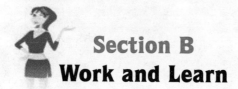

Section B
Work and Learn

Business Communication Skills

Leave a Positive First Impression

Whether you are aware of it or not, first impression does make a major difference in achieving business objectives. Having good manners will help you regardless of the business you are in. Any time you make contact with a client or a prospective client, you are making a mini-presentation of yourself, ultimately representing your company, service and/or products.

Address individuals by their honorifics or titles: The proper way to address a client is to greet him using his honorific or title followed by his last name. It is up to the client to ask you to call him by his first name. In business, the proper way to refer to a woman is "Ms.," regardless of her marital status.

Enunciate your greeting: Slow down and pronounce your name slowly, clearly and distinctly. At first it may feel as if you are exaggerating your name, but you are really helping the other person and improving overall communication.

Shake hands correctly: Extend your hand with the thumb up, clasp the other person's entire palm, give two or three pumps from the elbow, avoiding both the painful "bone crusher" and the off-putting "wet fish" shake, and look at the person directly in the eyes with a smile.

Smile: A smile shows that you like yourself; you like your current place in the world and you're happy with the people you're interacting with. A smile says, "I'm approachable and confident."

Make eye contact: Every time a person begins talking to you, look them in the eyes and smile first, then get on with the conversation. Also, when you enter a room for a meeting, smile and look around at everyone. If you want to start talking to one person, or even a group, come up to them and smile. Again, this is another way to say "I'm approachable."

Refer to individuals frequently by their names: Take the time and make the effort to pay attention to the name of the person you are being introduced to. A person's name means everything to him. To build rapport with a client, mention his name at least three times during the conversation. It will help you remember his name and make a connection.

Work Skills—Booth Personnel Skills

1 What do you know about booth personnel skills?

2 What shouldn't be done when you are working at a trade fair?

Words and Expressions

- ✓ booth
- ✓ exhibition hall
- ✓ sample
- ✓ brochure
- ✓ catalogue
- ✓ demonstration
- ✓ choose from
- ✓ keep in touch

Useful Sentence Patterns

- ✓ Good morning! Welcome to Canton Fair!
- ✓ It's an honor to meet you.
- ✓ Here is my name card.
- ✓ Won't you have a look at the catalogue and see what interest you?
- ✓ What about having a look at the samples first?
- ✓ If there is anything I can do for you, please let me know.
- ✓ Have you seen our exhibits?
- ✓ We have been in this line for twenty years.
- ✓ Take your time, please.
- ✓ Thank you for coming.
- ✓ Have a nice day!

Sample Dialogue

Lydia Wang (W) is the sales assistant of K&S Group. She is working at the 105ᵗʰ Canton Fair.
Eddie Collins (C) is the purchasing manager of Malaysia Maiya Group. He comes to the
booth.

W: Good morning! Welcome to our booth!

C: Good morning! I'm from Malaysia. This is my business card.

W: Glad to meet you, Mr. —er...

C: Collins. Eddie Collins.

W: Mr. Collins, my name is Lydia Wang and here is my card. I'll be very glad to be of help to you. Would you like to have a seat?

C: Thanks. I'm looking around for children's shoes.

W: Mr. Collins, would you like to have a closer look at our samples?

C: Later on, perhaps. Right now I'd like to have a good look at your brochure.

W: All right, sir. Would you like a cup of tea, please?

C: Yes, thank you.

W: Won't you have a look at the catalogue and see what interest you? This is a copy of our catalogue. It will give you a good idea of the products we handle.

C: We really need more specific information about your products.

W: What about having a look at the samples?

C: Yes, let's.

W: We have a wide selection of colors and designs. This is our newly developed product. Would you like to see it?

C: This design has got a real China flavor.

W: This is our latest style. It had been a great success at the last exhibition in Paris.

C: The product gives you an edge over your competitors, I guess.

W: Thank you. Yes, although it has only been on the market for a few months. It is really competitive in the world market.

C: I see. But, there's one problem.

W: What's that?

C: Price.

W: You mean the price? I don't think you have to worry about it. Our goods are sold at the lowest price.

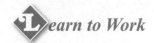 earn to Work

I. Try them in English

1. Words and Expressions

展位

展厅

样品

小册子

目录

示范

供挑选

保持联络

2. Sentences

早上好！欢迎来到广交会！

很荣幸认识您。

这是我的名片。

您愿意看看我们的目录吗？看看有什么您感兴趣的东西。

您先看看我们的产品陈列室好吗？

如果需要帮助，请告诉我。

您看过我们的展品吗？

我们在这一行已经做了二十年了。

请随意看。

谢谢光临。

祝您快乐！

II. Role-play

 Ella Black (B) is from American Hunters Company.

She comes to the booth. Lydia Wang, Ding Na's assistant, tries to get her name, title, interest and her schedule.

Lydia Wang is talking with Ella Black and shows her their products.

III. Dubbing

It's time for you to practice your spoken English for international business.

Conversation One

Conversation Two

Conversation Three

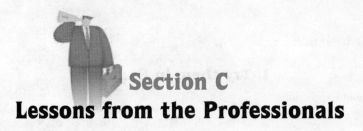

Section C
Lessons from the Professionals

Read the following article. There may be *some mistakes* in the use of English as well as in the operation or understanding of foreign trade. Discuss with your classmates and try to find some solutions to the problems concerning international trade.

Fair/Show Experience

AS EVERYBODY KNOWS THAT FAIR/SHOW IS THE MOST DIRECT WAY TO COMMUNICATE AND SHOW THE CLIENTS YOUR PRODUCT AND IT'S PRICE, AND IT HAS BEEN CONSIDERED THE BEST WAY TO FIND NEW CLIENTS AND GET MORE BUSINESS. I DON'T SAY THAT I HAVE MUCH EXPERIENCE FOR THAT, BUT JUST SHARE WITH YOU GUYS WHAT I HAVE LEARNT IN THE PAST DAYS, WISHING IT MAY GIVE YOU A HAND.

Firstly. Preparation before start.

1. Clothes. Check the recent weather situation for the fair/show places or countries in the internet and get ready for the proper clothes accordingly.

2. Notebook, pen, stapler, calculator, adhesive tape.
   notebook & pen—to write down the information talked with client
   stapler: to staple the business card
   calculator: to calculate the price if necessary
   adhesive tape: to seal the goods if you wanna sent back after the fair

3. Business card. normall take around 100pcs is enough, pls take more if you go for Canton fair.

4. Catalogue. around 150pcs, pls take more if you go for canton

5. Laptap if you have one, but I suggest to bring an interesting book with you which will help to let time pass easily in the evening.

Display goods in the booth.

1. Make sure to finish it before the appointed time.

2. Make the goods arranged that you can easier introduce to the client.

3. Make it as neat and tidy after the finished the display. Find out the restroom and canteen in your floor.

Third. On the Show.

Dressed up yourself decently and properly.

Never speak loudly and walk around even thought there is no vistors, you will pay for it and lose big fish any time if you did.

It is not necessary to ask for a passbying client to have a look, he will be in if having interest; of course, a smile and say hello is OK.

Never make fun and point to the guys who When the client visit, you should do as follows.

Take the notebook and pen with so that you can write down the information when you are talking.

Give him a catalogue with your business card and ask his business card at the first step, so that you can know which countries he/she is from,which you can find out the normal standard for the products that he/she need. Ask him to have a seat and look through the catalogue and pick out the product he has interesting and pass him/her the sample and have a look and quote the price, clearly and accurately, give him brief introduction of the products. Such clients is serious ones which you may make business easily. Of course, many like to have a look on samples directly on himself/ herself, go with him and give the necessary information if he/she asks. Remember to put on special mark on the clients who sit down and have a further talk with you. Just what said above, these ones are why we com here.

If there are many clients visit together, you may ask the other have a seat firstly and talk with them one by one.

After one day is over, turn around the notebook and recall what you have talked in the fair,it will help give a deep impression on the information. There are many other accident in the fair, you should try to slove them gentily and politely.

For the greenhand, maybe it is the first time for you to attend the fair and see such many foreigners, however, it is not necessary to be neverous, just get everything ready and act as kindly as you can and send the necessary information.

Attention: The most important thing is that you quote the price accurately!!! At least, I'd like to share three "much" that happen a lot in the fair.

Buyer: How much...

Seller: ...

Buyer: TOO much

Buyer: Thank you very much...,

Seller: You are welcome, 88

Buyer: Bay-bay.

Alexnee

Task Two On the Phone

任务二 电话邀约

Learning Objective

Be aware of the basic business telephone etiquette.
Be able to talk with your client over the telephone.

My Gains

Business etiquette	
Work skills	
Language skills	

My Problems

Business etiquette	
Work skills	
Language skills	

Section A
Movie Time

Watch the video clip and answer the question.

What does Chris do in order to save time in his working hours?

The Pursuit of Happiness

I would love to have the opportunity to discuss some of our products

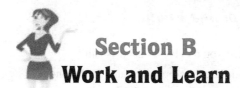

Section B
Work and Learn

Business Communication Skills

Mistakes in a Conversation (1)

Can you improve your conversation skills? Certainly. It might take a while to change the conversation habits ingrained throughout your life, but it is very possible. To not make this article longer than necessary, let's just skip right to the common mistakes many of us might have made in conversations, and a couple of solutions.

Not listening

Ernest Hemingway once said, "I like to listen. I have learned a great deal from listening carefully. Most people never listen." Don't be like most people. Don't just wait eagerly for your turn to talk. Put your own ego on hold. Learn to really listen to what people actually are saying. When you start to really listen, you'll pick up on loads of potential paths in the conversation. But avoid "yes" or "no" type of questions as they will not give you much information. If someone mentions that they went fishing with a couple of friends last weekend you can for instance ask:

- Where did you go fishing?
- What do you like most about fishing?
- What did you do there besides fishing?

The person will delve deeper into the subject giving you more information to work with and more paths for you choose from. If they say something like "Oh, I don't know" at first, don't give up. Prod a little further. Ask again. They do know, they just have to think about a bit more. And as they start to open up the conversation becomes more interesting because it's not on auto-pilot anymore.

Asking too many questions

If you ask too many questions the conversation can feel like a bit of an interrogation. Or like that you don't have that much to contribute. One alternative is to mix questions with statements. Continuing the conversation above you could skip the question and say:

- Yeah, it's great to just get out with your friends and relax over the weekend. We like to take a six-pack out to the park and play some Frisbee golf.
- Nice. We went out in my friend's boat last month and tried fishing.

And then the conversation can flow on from there. And you can discuss Frisbee golf or fishing.

Work Skills—Telephone Etiquette

1. What should you do when you receive a business call?
2. What will you say to your client before you hang up the phone?

Words and Expressions

- ✓ dial
- ✓ caller
- ✓ callee
- ✓ repeat
- ✓ hold on
- ✓ leave a message
- ✓ confirm
- ✓ itinerary

Useful Sentence Patterns

- ✓ Hello, this is Susan from K&S Group.
- ✓ May I speak to Li Ming, please?
- ✓ Just a moment, please.
- ✓ He's not available right now. Can I take a message?

✓ He wants you to call back as soon as possible.

✓ I call you today to ask if you are free tomorrow.

✓ Would it be possible to see you at 10:00 tomorrow morning?

S *ample Dialogue*

Ding Na (D) is sales manager of K&S Group. Eddie Collins calls for Ding Na for a discussion about his visit to the company.

Lydia Wang is Ding Na's assistant. Lydia puts him through.

W: Good morning, K&S Group.

C: Hello, this is Eddie Collins from Malaysia Maiya Group.

W: Hello, Mr. Collins. This is Lydia Wang. Very happy to hear you again.

C: Lydia! How is everything?

W: Fine, thank you. How may I help you?

C: Could I speak to Miss Ding Na, please?

W: Just a moment, please.

C: Thanks, Lydia.

W: Miss Ding, I have Eddie Collins on the line for you.

D: Thank you. Hello, Mr. Collins. Nice to hear from you. How's the weather like in Kuala Lumpur?

C: It's pretty good for the time of year. What's it like in Hangzhou?

D: Not good, I'm afraid. It's rather hot.

C: That's a pity because I'm planning to come across next week.

D: Really? Well, you'll come by to see us while you're here, I hope?

C: That's what I'm phoning about. I've got a meeting with a customer in Beijing on Thursday next week. I was hoping we could arrange to meet up either before or after.

D: Great. That would give us a chance to show you our new products and I can arrange a meeting for you and Mr. Young, our general manager.

C: That's what I was thinking.

D: So you said you have to be in Beijing on Thursday? That's the 10th?

C: That's right. Now, I could stop over in Hangzhou on Monday. Would that be possible?

D: OK. Well, it would be best for us if you could make it Monday morning. I will pick you up at the airport, and then you could meet Mr. Young and we'd show you around our company. If time permits, you could come back to the office and we'll run through any of the details that you are interested in.

C: That sounds good.

D: Look, why don't you fax me your information once you've confirmed your flight? Then we'll get back to you with an itinerary for the day — that's Monday, the 7th, right?

C: That's right. Well, I'll do that and I look forward to seeing you next week.

D: Same here. See you next week.

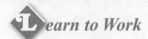 *earn to Work*

I. Try them in English

1. Words and Expressions

拨号

打电话的人

接电话的人

重复

拿着，别挂

留口信

确认

旅程

2. Sentences

Answering the phone

Asking to speak to someone

Asking someone to wait for a moment

Asking the caller to leave a message

Transferring information

Making an appointment

Suggesting a time

II. Role-play

 Ella Black wishes to talk about the contract with Ding Na.

Ding Na is in a meeting.

Lydia promises to tell Ding Na to call back.

 Ying Qiang (Y) is the sales manager of China Textiles Import and Export Co. Ltd.

He calls American Hunters Company.

He asks for Ella Black, the import manager.

He invites her to come for a visit.

III. Dubbing

It's time for you to practice your spoken English for international business.

Conversation One

Conversation Two

Conversation Three

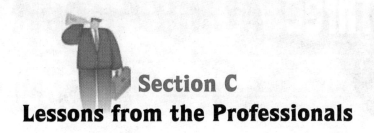

Section C
Lessons from the Professionals

Read the following article. There may be *some mistakes* in the use of English as well as in the operation or understanding of foreign trade. Discuss with your classmates and try to find some solutions to the problems concerning international trade.

6 Days Experience in the 102nd Canton Fair
fengyuan

2nd Day

More people visit our booth, I got many business card then put in the notebook, when I am free, I will write more details besides on the business card, even describe their image simply, it is a good way for us to get close to our customer, they hope can discuss business with familiar people, not stranger, sometimes I even record their length ^_^, which gave me a big favor later. My boss got a few cards by himself, then tell me details, asked me to write it down, my friend, Nicole, we help each other. To explain the difference between Chinese leather and Italian leather, I show our leather samples to the buyers, most of them are the experts, firstly they touch the leather by hand, smell it, some customers want to take a small leather away, but it is regret, we forgot to take forfex, then I write the message: do remember bring one forfex tomorrow.

To be excited, one important customer comes here, of course, I don't know he will be our kind customer, I regard him as usual visitor, ask for price, take the catalogue, he sit down, with one pen on his hand, open our catalogue, the action is absolutely same as other people, give me the items no that he is interested in, but I am so sorry, many people are in our booth at the same time, I offer him the price, go for other visitors, then back to him, again and again, many people didn't remember my name but him, he always called me Jessica, Jessica, come here? I have no time, please. a few minutes later, he left with our catalogue, I don't pay more attention to him, only get his name card.

Notes:

The 1st day:

http://forum.fobshanghai.com/viewthread.php?tid=315555&subject=6_days_experience_in_the_102nd_Canton_Fair&extra=&page=1

Task Three At the Airport

任务三 机场迎宾

Learning Objective

Be aware of the business etiquette of meeting a client.
Be able to meet your client at the airport.

My Gains

Business etiquette	
Work skills	
Language skills	

My Problems

Business etiquette	
Work skills	
Language skills	

Section A
Movie Time

Watch the video clip and answer the question.

What may Andrew call Margaret behind her back?

The Proposal

—见到你真好　—你让他喘不上气了，格瑞斯
— It's so good to see you! — you're suffocating him, grace.

Section B
Work and Learn

usiness Communication Skills

Mistakes in a Conversation (2)
Poor delivery

One of the most important things in a conversation is not what you say, but how you say it. A change in these habits can make a big difference since your voice and body language is a vital part of communication. Some things to think about:

- Slowing down. When you get excited about something, it's easy to start talking faster and faster. Try to slow down. It will make it much easier for people to listen to and understand.
- Speaking up. Don't be afraid to talk as loud as you need for people to hear you.
- Speaking clearly. Don't mumble.
- Speaking with emotion. No one listens for that long if you speak with a monotone voice. Let your feelings be reflected in your voice.
- Using pauses. Slowing down your talking plus adding a small pause between thoughts or sentences creates a bit of tension and anticipation. People will start to listen more attentively to what you're saying.
- Learn a bit about improving your body language as it can make your delivery a lot more effective.

Not having to be right

Avoid arguing and having to being right about every topic. Often a conversation is not really a discussion. It's a more of a way to keep a good mood going. No one will be that impressed if you "win" every conversation. Instead just sit back, relax and help keep the good feelings going.

Work Skills—Introducing Yourself

① What are the general rules for introduction?
② What are the ways to introduce yourself?
③ How to conduct a group introduction?

Words and Expressions

- ✓ pick sb. up
- ✓ jet lag
- ✓ luggage
- ✓ get airsick
- ✓ lobby
- ✓ reception desk
- ✓ information desk

Useful Sentence Patterns

- ✓ Excuse me, are you Eddie Collins from Malaysia?
- ✓ You must be our long-expected guest, Mark Davis.
- ✓ May I introduce myself?
- ✓ I hope you've had a pleasant journey.
- ✓ Did you have a good flight?
- ✓ How long did the flight take?
- ✓ It must be a very tiring trip.
- ✓ Hope you have an enjoyable/ pleasant/ nice stay here.
- ✓ May I help you with your luggage?
- ✓ How do you like the weather here?

Sample Dialogue

Monday, June 7, 2010

Eddie Collins comes to Hangzhou for a business visit. He arrives at Hangzhou International Airport. Ding Na meets him at the airport.

D: Excuse me. Aren't you Mr. Collins from Malaysia?

C: Yes, I am Eddie Collins, purchasing manager of Malaysia Maiya Group.

D: Nice to meet you, Mr. Collins. I'm Ding Na, sales manager from K&S Group. Welcome to Hangzhou. We've been looking forward to meeting you.

C: How do you do, Miss Ding. It's very kind of you to meet me at the airport.

D: You're welcome. Did you have a good journey?

C: Well, I've got a little airsick.

D: You must need a good rest after the flight. Let's go straight to the hotel.

C: That sounds a good idea.

D: May I help you with your luggage?

C: Thank you, Miss Ding, but I can manage it myself.

D: Ok. This way please, Mr. Collins.

C: It's a beautiful day, isn't it?

D: Yes, but it is said that it's going to rain this afternoon.

C: Does it rain often in Hangzhou?

D: Yes. It often rains in this season. Is this the first time you have come to Hangzhou, Mr. Collins?

C: Yes. I've heard a lot about Hangzhou and the West Lake in my country. I am very glad to get this chance for a visit.

D: Hope you enjoy your stay here.

Learn to Work

I. Try them in English

1. Words and Expressions

接 (某人)

时差（反应）

行李

晕机

前厅

接待处

问讯处

2. Sentences

请问您是美国来的艾拉·布莱克吗?

您一定是我们期待已久的客人——马克·戴维斯吧?

请允许我做一下自我介绍!

旅途愉快吧?

飞行途中还顺利吗?

飞行了多长时间?

想必旅途十分劳累吧?

我希望您这次在这儿过得愉快。

我能帮您拿行李吗?

您觉得这里的天气怎么样?

II. Role-play

 Ying Qiang (Y) is the sales manager of China Textiles Import & Export Corporation. Ying Qiang is meeting Ella Black (B) at the airport.

 Ying Qiang and his assistant Rae Zhang are meeting Mike Bush from ABC Company at the airport.

III. Dubbing

It's time for you to practice your spoken English for international business.

Conversation One

Conversation Two

Conversation Three

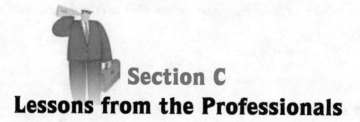

Section C
Lessons from the Professionals

Read the following article. There may be *some mistakes* in the use of English as well as in the operation or understanding of foreign trade. Discuss with your classmates and try to find some solutions to the problems concerning international trade.

My client is coming next week

SophiaLee2009

I have a client in Italy, he is coming to our factory to visit and see the production next week, and most likely to place order to me, which mentioned by today's email. So what should I do? What should I prepare before his coming? I have no experience.

Frank Brown (Frank)

congratulations first.

first,you can review your corespondences with this clients and pay attention to what he is interested in.

Then, make sure that you know well about the procedures and can tell the advantage of your products comparing with other opponents.

Next, to prepare the samples, files, quotation as well as negotiating documents.

I just think these tips, how they are useful for you.

bacon999

Support!

And it is better to prepare a small gift for the client.

qingtim99

For a newbie, product knowledge is the most important thing. Do some homework about your products. Stay calm and never be nervous when talking to clients. Impressing him with your professional knowledge and service would secure the order. Good luck.

Task Four At the Hotel

任务四 酒店入住

Learning Objective

Be able to help your client with the hotel check-in.

My Gains

Business etiquette	
Work skills	
Language skills	

My Problems

Business etiquette	
Work skills	
Language skills	

Section A
Movie Time

Watch the video clip and answer the question.

How can Chandler make his money back according to Ross?

Friends: The One with Rachel's Dream

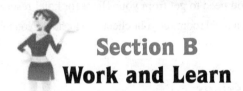

Section B
Work and Learn

usiness Communication Skills

How to Have a Business Conversation?

Perhaps you are new to the business world, or perhaps you have been in it for so long that you've lost your spark. Most sectors of the professional world require you to engage in formal business conversations. Even the most seasoned veterans can forget how to start a business conversation. Nevertheless, anyone can refer to the below steps for engaging in a painless, productive business conversation.

Step 1:

Get to know your business conversation partner. Learn more about your colleague by asking him how he is, where he comes from or some other benign but revealing questions.

Step 2:

Locate some common ground. Find out what similarities the two of you have, and then slowly move toward a more business-oriented conversation, where you can talk about what your companies or departments have in common as well.

Step 3:

Move toward topics such as the latest trends in your industry, your latest projects or whatever the predetermined topic of conversation is if you two are meeting for a specific reason.

Step 4:

Listen attentively to what your partner says, and respond with some quick comments throughout the business conversation, especially when other people love to talk. It's okay to give way to them in situations like this.

Step 5:

Compliment your conversation partner throughout the exchange. Who doesn't love to receive praise from time to time?

Step 6:

Make your own points in the business conversation in a firm but concise way. Everyone is short on time, and you don't want to cause any time management issues.

Step 7:

Close your business conversation with a firm handshake and a smile. Leave your partner with a positive and professional impression.

Work Skills—Hotel Reservation

1 What information do you need to get from your client for hotel reservation?

2 When you are reserving a hotel room for your client, what should you take into consideration?

Words and Expressions

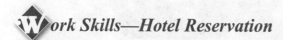

- ✓ registration
- ✓ porter
- ✓ baggage
- ✓ service charge
- ✓ suite
- ✓ double room
- ✓ twin room
- ✓ single room
- ✓ front desk
- ✓ receptionist
- ✓ service counter
- ✓ reception desk
- ✓ room (key) card

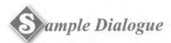seful Sentence Patterns

✓ What kind of room would you like?

✓ Would you like a single room or a twin / double room?

✓ Do you have a single room?

✓ Is there a room at the back of the hotel? I want a quiet room.

✓ I'd like a twin / double room with a bath.

✓ I'd like a single room with a view.

✓ Can I see the room, please?

✓ How long do you intend to stay?

✓ May I see your passport, please?

Sample Dialogue

Ding Na is helping Eddie Collins with his hotel check-in.

R: Good afternoon, sir. Good afternoon, miss. May I help you?

D: Yes. Is there a single room available, please?

R: Have you made a reservation?

D: Yes. For Eddie Collins. I called to reserve a single room two weeks ago.

R: Just a moment, Miss. I'll check on your reservation. Yes. We have you in our record.

R: Can I see your ID card or passport, Mr. Collins?

C: Sure, here you are.

R: Thank you, Mr. Collins. You'll have a single room on the top floor with a very good view of the West Lake.

C: Great! I like this room.

D: I'm glad you like it, Mr. Collins.

C: How much do you charge for the room?

R: We charge RMB 988 per night, plus 15 percent service charge. Will you please fill out the registration form, Mr. Collins?

C: Sure. Can I use my credit card?

R: Yes, we accept credit cards, including Master, Visa, Great Walls and Peony cards.

C: Good.

D: They have two restaurants. The Chinese one is on the second floor and the Western one is on the third floor.

C: Great. I'd like to try some Chinese food.

R: Your breakfasts are free of charge. Here are your breakfast coupons.

C: Thank you.

R: Have a nice stay!

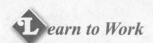
earn to Work

I. Try them in English

1. Words and Expressions

登记入住

行李员

行李

服务费

套房

双人房

单人房

前台

接待员

服务台

接待处

房卡

2. Sentences

您要什么样的房间？

您要单人房还是双人房？

你们有没有单人房间？

有没有靠后面的房间？ 我要一个安静的房间。

我想要一个带浴室的双人间。

我想要一个带风景的单人房间。

我看看房间行吗？

您打算住多久？

请出示您的护照。

II. Role-play

Ding Na has reserved two single rooms for Leona White (W) and Ella Hunter (H).

She is helping them with their check-in.

Leona White wants a quiet room.

Ella Hunter wants a room with a view.

Ying Qiang (Y) is checking in at a hotel.

He is heading a team of 30 members.

He asks for a discount.

III. Dubbing

It's time for you to practice your spoken English for international business.

Conversation One

Conversation Two
Conversation Three

Section C
Lessons from the Professionals

Read the following article. There may be *some mistakes* in the use of English as well as in the operation or understanding of foreign trade. Discuss with your classmates and try to find some solutions to the problems concerning international trade.

Do samples fee paid by your customer

Lisa1987710 (Lisa)

When customers tell you to send samples. the samples are free,but postage collect. it is our rules of my company.But why my customers always tell me to send samples all free, so upset. What your experience of sending samples,which one your choose.

1. the samples and the postage fee should be paid by customers

2. the samples be paid by customer but postage fee charged by your company

3. the samples are free,the postage fee paid by customer

4. all fee paid by your company

unique.chen

thats depend on the samples value,if the samples price is not high,we will send teh smaple for free but freight collect! and if the smaple is value so pay all fee please, you can told him thats our companys policy! if you send the sample free and express fee is free, they will think its easy to get sample, not treasure it,thats my humble opinion, just for your reference!

Lisa1987710 (Lisa)

tks. i know that, but customer tell you to send samples maybe it is a chance, if give up, you should wait for next chance...

Lisa1987710 (Lisa) if they don't want to pay, it means they don't have the sincere to cooperate with you?

Elaine9882 sure, sample is free, and the freight should be paid by customer, that's reasonable, cause so many clients ask for samples, if you pay for every one, what will happen? and if the client really want to buy products from you, he is willing to pay for the freight, we always operate in this way.

Notes:

postage collect 到付

e.g. The goods will be sent collect. 这个商品将根据货到收款来发送。

They sent us a collect message. 他们给我们传了封收到后付款的电报。

Task Five   Agenda

任务五 日程安排

Learning Objective

Be aware of the basic skills for making up an agenda.
Be able to discuss with the foreign visitors and decide on the agenda.

My Gains

Business etiquette	
Work skills	
Language skills	

My Problems

Business etiquette	
Work skills	
Language skills	

Section A
Movie Time

Watch the video clip and answer the question.

What is Sam's suggestion to Susan?

Family Album U.S.A.: Smell the Flowers

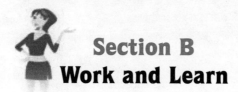

Section B
Work and Learn

usiness Communication Skills

Conversation Rules (1)

"People don't care how much you know, until they know how much you care."

— John Maxwell

Business conversations are a lot like any other kind of conversation, except that the polite topics are business and professional rather than personal and social. Usually, the purpose is to get acquainted with lots of people, exchanging pleasantries and facts with them, never monopolizing another person's time for the whole event.

Basic social conversation rules:
- Keep it short; keep the conversation moving. Limit responses to 60 seconds or less.
- Avoid opinion and emotion-evoking topics such as money, politics and religion.
- Do not interrupt.
- Do not finish other people's statements.
- If someone does or says something rude, ignore it.
- Do not complain.
- Do not criticize others. Say nothing evil about common acquaintances, former bosses or co-workers.

- Address a new acquaintance by his or her title and last name until you are invited specifically to use a first name.

Work Skills—Agenda Setting

① What must you take into consideration when you are drawing up an agenda?

② What kind of activities would be suitable for a visit?

Words and Expressions

✓ agenda
✓ rough schedule
✓ preference
✓ arrangement
✓ arrange
✓ business talks
✓ sightseeing
✓ comment
✓ convenience
✓ suit somebody
✓ first of all
✓ secondly
✓ and finally

Useful Sentence Patterns

✓ If you don't mind, let's discuss our agenda first.
✓ I'd like to talk with you about a couple of things on the agenda.
✓ We could go through them in order.
✓ Let's get down to business.
✓ I'm here to ask your opinion about the schedule of the next five days.
✓ I'd like to have your comments on the rough schedule.
✓ We'll leave some evenings free, if it is all right with you.
✓ If you have any questions on the details, feel free to ask.
✓ I wonder if it would suit you?
✓ In this case, I'll make some minor changes to meet your need.
✓ If possible, could you arrange a visit to your factory tomorrow?
✓ Any other business?

Sample Dialogue

Monday, June 7, 2010
It's half past two in the afternoon. Ding Na is discussing with Eddie Collins about the agenda.
Mr. Collins wishes to visit the factory that afternoon.

D: Good afternoon, Mr. Collins. Did you have a good rest?

C: Yes, I had a nap. I feel better now.

D: Very glad to hear that. Mr. Collins, I've drawn up a rough schedule for you during your stay here in Hangzhou. I'd like to talk with you about a couple of things on the agenda.

C: That's fine. If you could go through them in order, that'd be great.

D: You are going to stay in Hangzhou for three days. This evening there will be a welcome dinner party given in your honor and you will meet our general manager Young Gang there.

C: Thank you. I'm looking forward to meeting him. But what time would you like me to come?

D: The dinner will start at 5:30 p.m. I'll be at the hotel to pick you up at 5:00. Is the time convenient for you?

C: Yes, it's OK.

D: Good. Tomorrow we'll get down to our business negotiations. I hope we may reach a final agreement.

C: So do I.

D: We'll leave tomorrow evening free, if it is all right with you.

C: That's very considerate of you.

D: Since this is your first visit here, on the last day of your stay here, I'll show you around the city.

C: That's great.

D: If you have any questions on the details, feel free to ask.

C: Your schedule fits me very well. But could you arrange a visit to your factory this afternoon?

D: Of course, Mr. Collins. In this case, I'll show you around our factory and I'd like to show you our new products.

C: That'll be fine. Let's get moving.

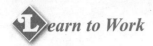 *earn to Work*

I. Try them in English

1. Words and Expressions

日程表

计划草稿

偏好

安排

安排商业洽谈

观光

评论, 意见

便利, 方便

2. Sentences

如果你不介意, 让我们先讨论我们的日程安排吧!

我想和你就日程安排进行交谈。

我们按顺序来讨论。

我们进入正题吧。

就接下来五天的日程安排,我特来征询一下您的意见。

我们想征询你对这份临时计划的意见。

如果你们愿意的话，我们想留几个晚上供你们自由支配。

如果对某些细节有意见的话，请提出来。

您看是否合适?

这种情况，我将稍做一些改变来满足你的要求。

如果可能的话，明天能否安排到你们工厂去参观?

还有什么别的事情吗?

II. Role-play

 Ding Na and Mr. Collins are talking about the agenda.

　　Mr. Collins wishes to go sightseeing.

　　Ding Na explains the day tour on the agenda.

Ding Na and Mr. Collins are talking about the agenda.

　　Mr. Collins wishes to visit the factory or to have a talk with some managers.

　　Ding Na agrees to make the arrangement.

III. Dubbing

It's time for you to practice your spoken English for international business.

Conversation One

Conversation Two

Conversation Three

Section C
Lessons from the Professionals

Read the following article. There may be *some mistakes* **in the use of English as well as in the operation or understanding of foreign trade. Discuss with your classmates and try to find some solutions to the problems concerning international trade.**

quarrel with my client
zora2006

one day, I got an inquiry and quote the price, a few days later, I send the samples. It's lucky, the client confirm our samples, and told me that he will give me a order. I'm so happy. But that's just the beginning. the quantity of the order is very small,which is different with we discuss before. Meanwhile, the price i quote is also for bulk production. then he also want us to give him commission which didn't mentioned before. At last, I find we can not do that price which already below our cost, I analyze it to my client,but he can not accept it. Then we quarreled with each other. Till now, still didn't find way to solve this problem.

-Lazy

Before give up, i think you may talk with him again. Keep your profit and persuade him to order. At least, let him know your price has been the best for your product. Maybe days later, he'll be back for your cooperation. Anyway, don't give up easily. Try and try again first. Business looks like a quarrel, quarrel for more profit.

jeff008

before his order, you should have a study of the customer background

is he a trader, wholesale, commission agent...?

cxcqingtian (Ivan)

Clam down, show your situation in detail. There is no need to quarrel with any clients whether he is big fish or small fish. There are so many demands in the international market, just find the sincere clients who really wanna do business with us with your most patience. If that customer is unworthy for you, just forget it.

Task Six Promotion

任务六 产品展示

Learning Objective

Have a good knowledge of the products and the company.
Be able to introduce your products to the visitor.

My Gains

Business etiquette	
Work skills	
Language skills	

My Problems

Business etiquette	
Work skills	
Language skills	

Section A
Movie Time

Watch the video clip and answer the question.

Does Chris do a good job in the demonstration?

The Pursuit of Happiness

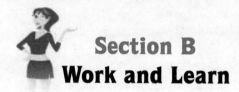

Section B
Work and Learn

usiness Communication Skills

Conversation Rules (2)

The Top Five most common topics of conversation, in order:

- Current events — Subscribe to and READ a business publication to have something to say.
- Sports — Even if you don't like sports, know what season it is and the names of the home town team.
- The event or job at hand — If you show up at any event, you need to know who sponsored it and why!
- The organization sponsoring the event — For newbies, asking others about the organization is a great conversation starter.
- Personal demographics — Where did you go to school, where do you live, how many kids do you have...

Conversation timing rules:

- At breakfast, business conversation can begin as soon as the coffee is poured.
- At lunch, make small talks until orders have been taken. Then you can talk business.
- At dinner, wait for the host to bring business into the conversation.

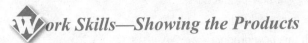ork Skills—Showing the Products

What must you do to make the promotion successful?

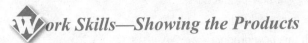ords and Expressions

- ✓ sample room
- ✓ meet one's satisfaction/ needs/ demands
- ✓ superior
- ✓ popular
- ✓ find a market
- ✓ selling line
- ✓ trial sale, test sale, test market
- ✓ capacity
- ✓ skillful
- ✓ microfiber
- ✓ genuine leather shoes
- ✓ casual boots
- ✓ sandals
- ✓ slippers
- ✓ sports shoes
- ✓ skillful manufacture
- ✓ unique style
- ✓ modern and elegant in fashion
- ✓ attractive and durable
- ✓ fashionable patterns

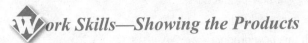seful Sentence Patterns

- ✓ Let me introduce this to you.
- ✓ Please take your time.
- ✓ What do you prefer?
- ✓ Do you have any special requirement?
- ✓ This is our newly developed products. Would you like to see it?
- ✓ Our company specializes in making high-quality children's shoes.
- ✓ This material has a durable and easy-to-clean surface.
- ✓ They are not only as low-priced as other makers, but they are distinctly superior in the following respects.

- ✓ You must be interested in seeing our new products.
- ✓ This product is the result of our latest technology.
- ✓ I'm sure you'll be satisfied with this new product.
- ✓ This product sells well in Europe.
- ✓ There is a great demand for this product.
- ✓ I'm convinced that this product will sell well.
- ✓ There is a good market for these articles.
- ✓ There is a poor market for these articles.
- ✓ There is no market for these articles.
- ✓ Our products are superior in quality and reasonable in price.
- ✓ Our products are the best sellers both in China and in the world.
- ✓ The natural material is the biggest feature of our products.

Sample Dialogue

After his visit to the factory, Eddie Collins comes to the show room.
Ding Na is showing him their products.

C: I'd like to have a look at the children's shoes you made. If the terms are favorable, we'll place an order.

D: We'll see what we can do. Shall we go to the showroom first where we can see the samples? These are casual boots with microfiber upper and EVA sole. Those are genuine leather shoes.

C: These genuine leather shoes are very special.

D: Yeah, they are most sellable in our market. They are formal and plain in color. The design is classic and elegant. The style is unique and the material is first-class, soft and springy.

C: Would you show me some more shoes?

D: All right. We produce various kinds of shoes, like sandals, slippers, sports shoes, and some special purpose shoes. We can offer you rich patterns.

C: We're interested in some of the styles here.

D: Shall we come to the office and talk about your requirements over a cup of tea?

C: Fine.

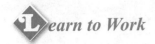earn to Work

I. Try them in English

1. Words and Expressions

样品室

有销路的

销路

试销

有技术的，熟练的

休闲鞋

超细纤维

真皮鞋

凉鞋

拖鞋

运动鞋

制作精良

风格独特

新颖大方

美观耐用

花色入时

2. Sentences

请慢慢看。

你喜欢什么样的？

这是我们新开发的产品，您要不要看一看？

我们公司专业生产优质童鞋。

这种材料经久耐用并且表面易清洁。

它们不仅价格低，与其他生产商相比，在以下方面显然更出众。

这种产品在欧洲非常畅销。

这种产品的需求量很大。

我确信这种产品一定会很畅销。

这些商品畅销。

II. Role-play

1 Miss Ella Black is looking for suppliers of children's shoes.

She comes to K&S Group for a visit.

Lydia Wang, Ding Na's assistant, is hosting her.

2 Ella Black and Lydia Wang are in the sample room.

Lydia is showing Miss Black their products.

III. Dubbing

It's time for you to practice your spoken English for international business.

Conversation One

Conversation Two

Conversation Three

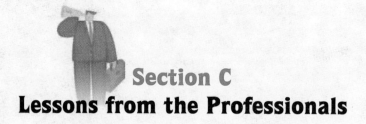

Section C
Lessons from the Professionals

Read the following article. There may be *some mistakes* in the use of English as well as in the operation or understanding of foreign trade. Discuss with your classmates and try to find some solutions to the problems concerning international trade.

How to Get Order

sophiaxie

I am working for a small company which is specialized in internet trade. As a sales, I believe the mission of all of people is get more and more orders. I also do it. But some times we found it is hardly make clients choose us after quotation, what shall we do? Give up or follow up? That is very importance. I would like to share one thing I met.

I got an inquiry from my USA client on last spring. At that time, he sent ten Price inquiries to Chinese supplier. Of course, I didn't know this thing at that time. I reply it and accompany with our pricelist in short time. At that time, he was satisfactory of our pricelist, and I thought that is no problem with our working together. And rest assured to do other things. After some days later, I found there was something wrong, my client hadn't send any information to us. What is the problem? I sent E-mail to him but he didn't reply it. That made me some worried. But I still went on send E-mail to him. Thank goodness, he replied it and told me there is a price from one factory is lower than us. That was a bad news to us. My client sent the price to me and asked me whether we should do as the same price. That was a factory owner and they wanted to got the order to give the factory's price. It is impossible in us because we are trading company, we can't do business without any profit. At the same time, we can't reduce our price to make our client thought there is a big profit with us, so I refused but I analyzed each cost in this produce treatment. Of course, I showed the price which that factory offered is not possible but I didn't say any bad word on that factory, in the end, I said: wish you have a good working with. My client was very surprised and told to me: Jessica, you are so professional. We will do other business with you because most of our directorates had choose that factory. And I will contact you if there is something wrong with this factory. After read that, there was some disappointment but I saw some hope.

I still sent the E-mail to him each week but there was no any information. After three months later, I surprised to saw his letter. OMG, that was really good news to us! He told me: Jessica, I would like to do business with you, please send the price for us! What a surprise am I! I got an opportunity from him. And at this time, he hadn't sent any inquiry to other suppliers. That is really a nice chance.

I must say I am met him at good time and good place. But I believe everyone would meet client like this. But have you catch the chance? What are you doing at that time? Are you follow up? Good time and good place is very important but the thing is, you must more professional than your client and follow up. And I believe it will win one day.

Task Seven At the Company

任务七 公司接待

Learning Objective

Be aware of the basic rules of reception.
Be able to provide necessary information to visitors.
Be able to make arrangements for visitors.

My Gains

Business etiquette	
Work skills	
Language skills	

My Problems

Business etiquette	
Work skills	
Language skills	

Section A
Movie Time

Watch the video clip and answer the question.

What will Mr. Sakai do during his visiting?

Starting Business English: Receiving Visitors

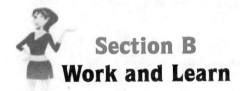

Section B
Work and Learn

usiness Communication Skills

Appearance

It can be insulting to your co-workers or clients to show a lack of concern about your appearance. Make sure that your clothes fit physically and that they fit the occasion and the setting. If in doubt, always err on the side of conservative. Be clear about how you expect people to look for your business. Business casual dress remains more formal than what you'd wear at home. Wearing wrinkled clothes or arriving smelly and unkempt communicates that you don't care enough about the situation, the people, or the company to present yourself respectably.

Business suit and tie are appropriate in all major cities. Wear dark colored business suits in classic colors of gray and navy. For an important formal meeting, choose a white dress shirt, for less formal a light blue shirt will still give you a conservative appearance. Women should wear a suit or dress with jacket in major cities. Wearing classic clothing and classic colors of navy, gray, ivory, and white will ensure that you give a confident and conservative appearance.

Work Skills—Reception Skills

What makes a pleasant reception?

Words and Expressions

- ✓ president (of a company)
- ✓ president of the board
- ✓ chief executive
- ✓ business executive
- ✓ vice-president
- ✓ director
- ✓ manager
- ✓ sales manager
- ✓ short visit
- ✓ show sb. around
- ✓ conference room

Useful Sentence Patterns

- ✓ What can I do for you? / How can I help you?
- ✓ May I have your name, please?
- ✓ What company are you from?
- ✓ Could you tell me what company you are representing?
- ✓ Do you have an appointment?
- ✓ Would you like something to drink?
- ✓ Please wait a moment.
- ✓ I have an appointment with…
- ✓ He isn't here. Can you leave a message?
- ✓ How do you do?
- ✓ It's an honor for me to meet you.
- ✓ I'm pleased to meet you.
- ✓ I've often heard so much about you.
- ✓ Mr. Smith often talked about you.

Sample Dialogue

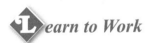

Tuesday, June 8, 2010
Eddie Collins comes to K&S Group for his appointment with Ding Na.
Li Lin, office secretary, receives him.

L: Good morning, sir. How can I help you?

C: Good morning! I am Eddie Collins from Malaysia Maiya Group. I'd like to see Miss Ding.

L: Do you have an appointment?

C: Yes. Our meeting is at 8 o'clock.

L: I'm wondering if Miss Ding forgot your meeting. I am afraid she left her office this morning and she is not expected back until 10. Let me find out if she had made an arrangement for someone else to meet with you in her place. Will you please have a seat?

C: Sure.

L: Would you like something to drink?

C: No, thank you.

L: Yeah, Mr. Collins, I just checked with our office manager Miss Terry. She said Miss Ding briefed her on your project. She is just finishing up our meeting now. She would be meeting you shortly. Would you like me to show you around for your waiting?

C: That would be very nice. Thank you!

L: Right this way, Mr. Collins. We can start with our front office. When Miss Terry is ready, you may go up there to the conference room on the 6th floor.

Learn to Work

I. Try them in English

1. Words and Expressions

总经理/总裁

董事长

总经理，主管

业务主管

副总经理

主任或部门负责人

经理

销售经理

短期访问

带某人参观

会议室

2. Sentences

先生，有什么需要吗？

请问您的名字是？

您是哪个公司的？

能告诉我您代表什么公司吗？

您有预约吗？

想喝些什么吗？

请稍等。

我与XX有个约会。

他不在，需要留言吗？

你好。

见到您非常荣幸。

很高兴能认识您。

久仰大名。

史密斯先生经常提到您。

II. Role-play

 Ella Black comes for a visit to China Textile Import and Export Company. Ying Qiang receives her in the office.

Ella Black has an appointment with Ying Qiang. She comes to the company for the visit. Ying Qiang receives her.

III. Dubbing

It's time for you to practice your spoken English for international business.

Conversation One

Conversation Two

Conversation Three

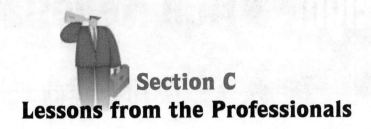

Section C
Lessons from the Professionals

Read the following article. There may be *some mistakes* in the use of English as well as in the operation or understanding of foreign trade. Discuss with your classmates and try to find some solutions to the problems concerning international trade.

What should I do?

<u>tanchunyu89</u>

Hello, everybody! This is Sophia, I find one E-mail from the record of the customer as follows,

MR. VEROLI, WHO IS RESPONSIBLE TO FOLLOW THIS KIND OF BUSINESS, HAS JUST ASKED ME TO INFORM YOU THAT WE ARE NOT INTERESTED IN BUSINESS RELATIONSHIP WITH YOUR COMPANY IN THE FUTURE.

WE DID NOT APPRECIATE THE PREVIOUS BUSINESS RELATIONSHIP WITH YOUR COMPANY IN THE PAST. SO PLEASE DO NOT CONTACT US ANY MORE.

REGARDS

It is apparent that our company has a unpleasant cooperation with this customer. And I did not involve this business before, because I have not coem to this company at that time. What should I do? I have sent many Emials to this customer. but there is no reply. Hope you cna give me some suggestions.

Frank Brown

Look for all correspondences / transactions with this clients to know the cause and effect, then make a decision. we know nothing about you and this customer, so the suggestion is meanless.

qingtim99

Sometimes we have to learn how to give up. Just let go or your insisting may offend him and make things worse. Belief outweigh gold, seemingly your company have lost that thing outweighing gold in your customer's mind. To win back it I am afraid you got to work harder 10 times. Never put all the eggs in only one basket. Don't waste your time and energy, instead using you time and energy to look for a new one. It makes sense and don't worry, there are lots of big fish out there awaiting for you.

lily trade

If i were you, I will check with our company about the cooperation history with that customer to confirm what happened before. Then tell him you don't know what happened before cuz you are a new comer in this company, but you have checked the whole things. That would be better to make a apologize to them if it was our company's problem, also tell him we have tried solve the prolem & will never happened again, meantime, whenver he need our help, just feel free to contact us.

Task Eight Price Negotiation

任务八 谈判与磋商——价格

Learning Objective

Be aware of the basic skills for price negotiation.
Be able to talk with the client about the price.

My Gains

Business etiquette	
Work skills	
Language skills	

My Problems

Business etiquette	
Work skills	
Language skills	

Section A
Movie Time

Watch the video clip and answer the question.

What is Mr. McNeil's mark-up on Big Boss?

Starting Business English: Negotiating Prices (1)

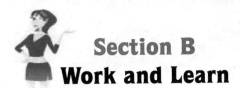

Section B
Work and Learn

Business Communication Skills

The Importance of Good Communication in Organizations

Good communication skills are imperative for any business. In fact, these skills can often mean the difference between success and failure.

Lee Iacocca, former president of Chrysler, once said, "You can have brilliant ideas, but if you can't get them across, they won't get you anywhere." Iacocca was absolutely right, and his sage words of advice apply to both personal and business communication.

Communication is vital in an organization because it not only connects members within a specific department but also connects them to members from other departments, from other branches, and, in today's global economy, from around the world. Moreover, communication can make the difference between success and failure for a company.

Good communication helps ensure the efficient operation of all levels of an organization, from lowest to highest, whereas poor communication often results in inefficiency; and as successful business leaders know, inefficiency equals a loss of productivity and, consequently, a loss of profits.

Work Skills—Price Negotiation

What will you do in order to get the upper hand in a price negotiation?

Words and Expressions

- ✓ quote
- ✓ price list
- ✓ discount
- ✓ inquire
- ✓ tax
- ✓ offer
- ✓ firm offer
- ✓ official offer
- ✓ wholesale price
- ✓ retail price
- ✓ concession
- ✓ reduction
- ✓ deal

Useful Sentence Patterns

- ✓ How much is this?
- ✓ How much does it cost?
- ✓ What is the price, please?
- ✓ Can you give me your favorable price?
- ✓ What's your best quotation?
- ✓ Could you please give me your offer for this kind of goods?
- ✓ Could you offer us your best price?
- ✓ Is tax included?
- ✓ Please quote 2000 pcs of sweaters FOB Shanghai.
- ✓ Please quote ten cartons of green tea CIF Vancouver, including 5% commission.
- ✓ Can we both make some concession?
- ✓ I'll take it if you give me a 20% discount.
- ✓ Can I have your price list?
- ✓ Will you give us an indication of prices?
- ✓ What about the prices?
- ✓ Our price is realistic and based on reasonable profit.

✓ If an order is placed, we'll pay the cost of the sample.

✓ It is rather beyond our expectation.

✓ What would be your lowest price for your product?

✓ That's far more costly than I expected.

✓ Your prices are beyond our expectation.

✓ The price is much on the high side.

✓ The price is beyond our reach.

✓ The price is rather out of line.

✓ I'm afraid I can't agree with you there.

✓ This is our wholesale price/ retail price/ producer's price.

✓ This is our lowest price.

✓ The price has been reduced to the limit.

✓ There is no room for reducing price.

✓ This price is as low as we can go.

✓ Our products/ goods are excellent/ high in quality and reasonable/ cheap in price.

✓ Can you give me a discount?

✓ Your price is too high and we ask for a reduction of 5%.

✓ Let's meet each other half way. I have to call the deal off if you can't accept the price.

✓ We may as well call the deal off.

✓ Perfect! That's a deal!

✓ You certainly have a way of talking me into it.

✓ We are prepared to accept your offer.

✓ We accept the offer you made on May 16th.

✓ Deal!/ Done!

Sample Dialogue

Tuesday, June 8, 2010

Eddie Collins is interested in some of the products and he is negotiating with Ding Na about the price.

D: Good afternoon, Mr. Collins.

C: Good afternoon, Miss Ding.

D: Are you satisfied with our samples? Shall we move on to the next step?

C: Yes, I'm interested in some of them. I have an inquiry for leather shoes. Please offer your lowest prices for this style of children's genuine leather shoes. Lining material is genuine leather, outsole material rubber and upper cowhide.

D: All right, but could you tell us how many do you want?

C: How about the minimum quantity you require?

D: For this kind of high-quality shoes, the minimum quantity should be at least 500 pairs.

C: I see, we'd like to order 600 pairs for this kind, so your lowest price?

D: Ok, let me see. The price should be at USD16.6/pair FOB Shanghai.

C: I know your research costs are high, but what I'd like is a 15% discount.

D: That seems to be a little high, Mr. Collins. I don't know how we can make a profit with those numbers.

C: I believe we could order a lot more if you would agree to reduce prices by 15%.

D: Mr. Collins, material for genuine leather is in short supply this year, and the price is changeable quickly. It would be very difficult to reduce them by 15%.

C: I'm afraid I can't agree with you there. You know there is keen competition in the market in this special time. Many suppliers earn no money because of financial crisis.

D: That's true, but our goods are in high quality. It is worthy of the price. Anyhow, the price we've offered is in line with the market. This is our rock-bottom price. We can't make any further concession.

C: If that's the case, we will call off the deal.

D: Well, considering our first business and long-term cooperation, let's meet each other half way.

C: You mean?

D: I mean we can only make a reduction of 8%. That is for the order of 600 pairs at USD15.3/pair FOB Shanghai. That's definitely rock-bottom.

C: Ok, thank you. I will pass this information on to my boss and let you know the results at an early time.

C: Ok.

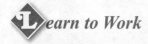

L earn to Work

I. Try them in English

1. Words and Expressions

报价
价目表
折扣
询价,询问
税, 税款
报盘
实盘
正式报价
批发价
零售价
让步

减少, 缩减量

交易

2. Sentences

这个多少钱?

能给我优惠的价格吗?

你方最底报价是多少?

请报这种产品的价格。

你能报最低价吗?

含税吗?

请报2000件针织衫上海离岸价。

请报十箱绿茶温哥华到岸价，包括5%的佣金。

双方各让一步好吗?

如果你打八折，我就要了。

你能给我价格单吗?

我们的价格是很实际的，是根据合理的利润提出的。

假如交易成功，样品费由我们付。

这太出乎意料。

这比我预料的要贵得多。

你方报价超出了我们的预期。

价格太高了。

价格我们不能接受。

价格与当前行市不符。

在那个方面，恐怕我不能同意你的意见。

这是我们的批发价/ 零售价/ 出厂价。

该报价已经降到最低限了。

没有降价的空间了。

这个价格是我们能报的最低价。

我们的产品物美价廉。

能打折吗?

你公司报价太高，我们要求减价5%。

让我们各让一步。这个价格如果你们还不能接受，那我只好取消这个交易。

我们干脆放弃这笔交易好了。

太棒了！成交!

你真有一套。

我们接受贵公司5月16日的报盘。

成交!

II. Role-play

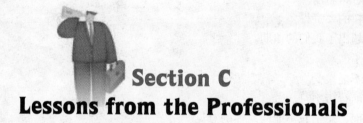

Ella Black and Lydia Wang are talking about the order and price.

Ella Black inquires for 1000 pairs of children's leather shoes.

She asks for a 20% discount.

Lydia agrees to give her a 10% discount.

Ella Black and Lydia Wang are talking about the order and price.

Ella Black inquires for 1000 pairs of children's leather shoes.

She urges a 10% discount.

Lydia Wang agrees on a 6% concession.

III. Dubbing

It's time for you to practice your spoken English for international business.

Conversation One

Conversation Two

Conversation Three

Section C
Lessons from the Professionals

Read the following article. There may be *some mistakes* in the use of English as well as in the operation or understanding of foreign trade. Discuss with your classmates and try to find some solutions to the problems concerning international trade.

how can I let the customer know I have offered the best price?

lianshangyu1986

I have an India customer. We have talked about the price for about 2 weeks. And I have gave him the best price but he still want a lower price. And I am tired with talking the price with him. I don't know how to do. Can someone tell me how I can let him place the order?

musa

Every buyer want to catch any cheapest possibility, and every seller do want to offer higher. that's human. ...it's difficult to balances. I dont want to promise that our prices is cheapest in the world, but the truth is our product worth the prices. if we dont trust each other, how could us to go ahead our cooperation. please think about it and be appreciated for your understanding.

huangxiang5091

you can ask him to know more about your maket then he really know your price is really reasonable ...the customer talked about the price for about 2 weeks with you and i think the customer is really want to establish business relationship with you

wondersway

All the india Clients I have met is all more less the same, They always want the lowest price, It is related to the Economy developement and marketing policy of that country. If the client always bargain the price with you, It means he is paying great attention to the case, And I guess the price you have offered him is reasonable, maybe he is in the process of double checking the price with other suppliers to see whether he can get a better price or not. Hold on and wait!

smithereens

I think you don't need give the real price to the customer in your first email.f

Because almost half past customers don't believe your first price, they will bargain over the price with you in the next several emails.

gracegu

india customers always say your price is high. almost each time i send them quotation, their reply is: your price is on higher side... even i send them our best price.

Task Nine Packing Negotiation

任务九 谈判与磋商——包装

Learning Objective

Be aware of the basic packing knowledge.
Be able to go over the details of the packing of goods with your client.

My Gains

Business etiquette	
Work skills	
Language skills	

My Problems

Business etiquette	
Work skills	
Language skills	

Section A
Movie Time

Watch the video clip and answer the question.

How do Dan and Carter persuade Kalb into advertising with Sports America magazine?

In Good Company

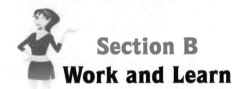

Section B
Work and Learn

usiness Communication Skills

External and Internal Communication

Increased efficiency isn't the only result of good communication, however, since it also creates a sense of unity between members, resulting in their feeling that they are working together toward a common goal, and that goal is the success of the organization.

There are two categories of communication within an organization: external and internal.

External Communication involves the transfer of information either to or from individuals outside the organization, and the goal of this type of communication is often to obtain a favorable response to the organization's needs. For example, a company might send a sales advertisement to an existing customer or a proposal, prospectus, or solicitation to a potential client; or an organization might post an ad in hopes of attracting qualified applicants for a job vacancy.

Internal Communication involves the transmittal of information between individuals within the company, and its aim is usually to accomplish internal objectives. For example, management might let employees know when and how a particular task should be completed, or employees might ask for clarification of the specifics for a task. Additionally, management might suggest improvements to products or services, or employees might present their qualifications when asking for a promotion or pay increase.

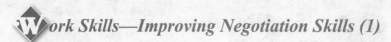

ork Skills—Improving Negotiation Skills (1)

What is your understanding of the two skills, to compromise and to be fair?

ords and Expressions

- ✓ pack
  - ■ to be packed in paper bag
  - ■ single packing
  - ■ collective packing
  - ■ outer packing
  - ■ inner packing
  - ■ packing charge
  - ■ packing clause
- ✓ package
- ✓ intact
- ✓ tastefully
- ✓ well-done
- ✓ to be on a par with
- ✓ unique
- ✓ rough handling
- ✓ reinforce
- ✓ to reinforce the packing
- ✓ case
  - ■ carton
  - ■ wooden case
  - ■ crate
  - ■ chest
  - ■ box
  - ■ plastic bag
  - ■ foam plastic bag
  - ■ canvas
  - ■ bundle
  - ■ can/tin
  - ■ glass jar
  - ■ container
  - ■ pallet
- ✓ proof
  - ■ breakage-proof

- shake-proof
- leakage-proof
- water-proof
- sound-proof

✓ mark

- indicative mark
- warning mark
- Upward
- This Side Up
- Handle with Care
- Keep Upright
- Use No Hooks
- Not to Be Tripped
- Keep in a Dry Place
- Keep away from Heat
- Keep away from Cold
- Keep Dry
- Explosive
- Fragile
- Inflammable
- Inflammable Gas

Useful Sentence Patterns

✓ Do you have specific request for packing? Here are the samples of packing available now, you may have a look.

✓ How is … packed? …

✓ I'd like to have a look at the pack. Have you got any samples?

✓ We usually pack the goods in cardboard boxes, 100 boxes to one carton.

✓ The outer packing should be suitable/ strong enough for long-distance ocean transportation.

✓ Packing charge is already included in the price.

✓ Packing charge is about 5% of the total cost of the goods.

✓ How much will the new packing add to the cost price?

✓ Usually, we use two languages on the labels—English and French.

✓ The packing must be strong enough to withstand rough handling.

✓ We have especially reinforced our packing in order to minimize the extent of any possible damage to the goods.

✓ The charges of packing are usually born by buyers.

✓ You must mark "Handle with Care" on the face of the box.

✓ The Side Up.

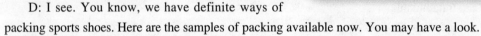

✓ Bar codes should be marked on the inner packing.

𝓢ample Dialogue

Tuesday, June 8, 2010
Ding Na and Eddie Collins are negotiating about the packing of the goods.

C: The next thing I'd like to bring up for discussion is packing.

D: Do you have specific request for packing?

C: The outer packing should be strong enough for transportation. As to inner packing, it must be attractive and helpful to the sales.

D: A wrapping that catches the eyes will certainly help push the sales.

C: We require the goods should be packed one pair in one shoe box, one size into one export carton, 12 pairs in one export carton.

D: I see. You know, we have definite ways of packing sports shoes. Here are the samples of packing available now. You may have a look.

C: Great! We will give you the packing instruction later.

D: That is wonderful.

C: We wish our opinions on packing will be passed on to your manufacturers. You know, packing has a close bearing on sales.

D: Yes, it also affects the reputation of our products. Buyers always pay great attention to packing. We wish the new packing will give our clients satisfaction.

C: Ding, since you will use the new packing, how much is it?

D: It's about 5% of the total cost of the goods. It's included in the price.

C: I agree. You will follow the packing instruction strictly.

D: Please rest assured.

𝓛earn to Work

I. Try them in English

1. Words and Expressions

包装，装罐

包装方法

完整的，未损伤的

精美的，高雅的

美观，讲究

与……相媲美

独特的

粗暴装运

加强，增援

唛头

2. Sentences

你们对包装有什么特别要求吗？这是我们目前用的包装样品，你可以看一看。

……产品怎么包装？

我想看看包装，你们有样品吗？

我们通常用纸盒包装货物，一百盒装一纸箱。

外包装必须坚固利于长途海运。

包装费用已包括在价格中。

包装费大约占货物总成本的5%。

用新包装成本费用要增加多少？

通常我们在标签上使用两种语言：英语和法语。

包装必须十分坚固，以承受粗暴的搬运。

我们已经特意加固包装，以便使货物万一遭到的损坏减小到最低程度。

包装费用通常是由买方承担的。

贵公司必须在箱子的正面注明"小心轻放"。

此端向上。

条形码应该标在内包装上。

II. Role-play

Ella Black inquires for 1000 pairs of children's leather shoes.

Lydia Wang and Ella Black are talking about the packing of the goods.

Ella Black requires cardboard boxes for the packing.

III. Dubbing

It's time for you to practice your spoken English for international business.

Conversation One

Conversation Two

Conversation Three

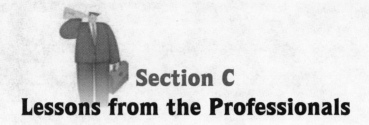

Section C
Lessons from the Professionals

Read the following article. There may be *some mistakes* in the use of English as well as in the operation or understanding of foreign trade. Discuss with your classmates and try to find some solutions to the problems concerning international trade.

Finally make a deal!
<u>jmk168</u>

From August to now, i am writing with my USA customers for about 5 months. Finally i make a deal with him.

ust like all enquiries, I explain every detial of our products to him and quoate... After several mails, the put our products's pictures to his website and start to promote our products. I am so happy. I have thought that he place an order soon or later... But time passes by, no order! Even though we have talked about samples... but Chinese milk affair affect it a lot! He said him customer do not trust make-in-china products any more... So Sample is blocked. Actually i am trying my best to let him believe supre-quality of our products. As usaual, i send him email and say hello. But our deal does not make any progress.

I am almost lost my heart. For near one month, i can not hear from him. I really think that there is no hope. But one day i recieve a mail from him. He said that he wanted some samples. I am so happy. Of course, email him everyday to sovle all the problems including, price, products specification, shipping etc. Oh, no way to go. FOB Business.

At last they wire 30% payment to our company, so happy again! But i am also worried about it.Because still there are some problems unsettled, Especially shipping. On the one hand, i should gurantee our company recieve the rest of payment. On the other hand, i should make my customer trust me. One one would like to take risk.

At this time, our customers think our price is a little hiher and he can only make a little profit. So i do not know what he is thinkin about. I email him, but no reply. This monring i hear from him. He said freight fee is very high through UPS, paid by his UPS account. if so, he will have no profit. I can really understand him. He asks me to give him suggestions. I consult some Express Company. To my surprise, freight fee is just half of that he pay by his UPS account.

I email him, so he accept and he said he see some profit. He is really happy, me too. He said he trust me and wire money to the account of our company tommorrow! Finally i make a deal by myself. i feel acheived.

So I think, order will be sooner or later only if you serve customer soul and heart.

Task Ten Transport Negotiation

任务十 谈判与磋商——运输

Learning Objective

Be aware of the basic transport knowledge.
Be able to go over the details of the goods transportation with your client.

My Gains

Business etiquette	
Work skills	
Language skills	

My Problems

Business etiquette	
Work skills	
Language skills	

Section A
Movie Time

Watch the video clip and answer the question.

What is their final agreement on delivery?

Starting Business English: Negotiating Delivery

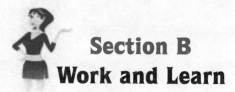

Section B
Work and Learn

Business Communication Skills

Habits of Communication

Learning to communicate effectively is a life-long process. Often it is a combination of trial and error and learning the hard way. This process contributes—sometimes positively and at other times negatively—to perceptions of ourselves and others. Patterns and habits of communication develop from childhood and are carried well into adulthood and old age. These habits are so subconscious that much of the time we have no realistic idea of how we are perceived by others.

People communicate in the best way they know and do not realize when and how they are failing to convey their intended message. When it is understood that the message is not clear, it is not a matter of blaming the past or making excuses; rather, it involves the maturity to recognize and change the elements of your communication that are not serving you well for those that are more effective. It is a matter of saying or thinking: No matter what has happened in the past, do I want this pattern or behavior now? It is my choice to behave, react, respond differently and now I choose to do it another way. Past is past; I cannot go on behaving the way I have in the past and expect anything other than the responses I evoked in the past. There is a saying: When you think the way you have always thought, you will act the way you have always acted and you will get what you have always got.

Work Skills—Improving Negotiation Skills (2)

1 Why is listening important in negotiation?

2 Please list some good listening techniques.

Words and Expressions

✓ Transport:

- transportation
- transportation business
- transportation company (corporation)
- transportation cost
- mode of transportation
- transportation by sea, land, air, and mail
- combined transportation
- to be in transit
- move
- cargo space
- Train-Air-Truck (TAT;TA)

✓ Documents:

- transport document
- shipping documents
- Bill of Lading (B/L)

✓ Terms of shipment:

- forward shipment
- near shipment
- prompt shipment
- shipment as soon as possible
- load time
- initial shipment
- partial shipment
- transshipment/ transhipment
- transhipment prohibited

✓ Ports:

- loading port
- unloading port
- port of shipment
- port of destination

Useful Sentence Patterns

✓ Is there any way to make an earlier shipment?

✓ Can't you make shipment 10 days earlier?

✓ Please try your best to ship one forth of the goods prior to the shipment.

✓ We can advance the shipment. / We can ship the goods in advance. But you must open the L/C ahead of time.

✓ We agree to transshipment at HK.

✓ Please insure the goods on our account during transshipment.

✓ Please note in the L/C "Partial Shipment Allowed."

✓ We require that goods should be shipped during Aug. and Sep. in two monthly lots.

✓ We require that transshipment be allowed.

✓ When can you make shipment?

✓ We'll get the goods dispatched within the stipulated time.

✓ I wonder if you could ship the order as soon as possible?

✓ Let's discuss about the mode of transportation.

✓ What mode of transportation do you suggest we use?

✓ What sort of delivery periods did you have in mind?

✓ For such a big order, we propose to have the goods dispatched by sea.

✓ Because of the high cost of railway transportations, we prefer sea transportation.

✓ Sometimes sea transport is troublesome to us.

✓ Please have the goods transported by air.

✓ Can you have them sent by railway?

✓ We think it necessary to move the articles by way of combined transportation.

✓ I don't like this kind of combined transportation.

✓ It's easy to cause a delay in shipment or even lose the goods completely when we arrange such combined transport.

✓ Who will bear the extra freight charges?

✓ Freight for shipment from Shanghai to Hongkong is to be charged to your account.

✓ The bill of lading should be marked as "freight prepaid."

✓ You may choose Beijing as port of shipment.

✓ We'd like to designate Shanghai as the loading port because it is near the producing area.

✓ What's your unloading port please?

✓ We'd like to change the unloading port from Kuching to Melaka.

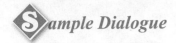

Sample Dialogue

Tuesday, June 8, 2010
Ding Na is negotiating with Mr. Collins about the time of shipment.
Eddie Collin wishes to have the goods shipped at an earlier date.
They agree on a partial shipment.

D: I am glad we have settled the questions of quality, quantity, packing and price. Shall we go on with the shipment?

C: Sure. When can you effect shipment?

D: We usually effect shipment within 2 months after we've received your L/C. We can effect shipment in September at the latest.

C: I'm terribly worried about late shipment. September is the selling season for these goods. Is there any way to make an earlier shipment?

D: I can't say "yes" now. As I said, raw material is hot. I can't promise the earlier shipment.

C: Do you have any suggestion? It is the selling season. September shipment is too late.

D: Let me see. If possible, will you accept half of the goods prior to the rest of the shipment?

C: When could you send the first lot?

D: By the end of August?

C: Ok.

D: How are you going to handle the shipping? By air or by sea?

C: Could you send it by air please?

D: Ok. Do you want us to use our freight forwarding agent?

C: Actually, we've got a freight forwarder. I'll fax you their contact information.

D: That would be great. I'll let you know the shipping details later and send you the shipping documents by DHL as soon as I get them.

C: Very good. We'll be expecting to hear from you.

earn to Work

I. Try them in English

1. Words and Expressions

运输
运输方式
海运

联运

运输单据

第一批货

分批装运

转运

装运港

目的港

2. Sentences

有没有办法提前装运?

贵公司能否提前十天装运呢?

请尽量在装运前发运四分之一的货物。

我们可以提前装运,但是贵公司必须提前开出信用证。

我们同意在香港转运。

转运期间,请给这批货物投保,费用由我方承担。

请在信用证注明"允许分批装运"。

我们要求贵公司在8月和9月分两批装运。

我们将按规定的时间发货。

我们讨论一下运输方式吧。

因为铁路运输费用高,我们愿意走海运。

有时海运对我们来说麻烦。

我们认为联运货物十分必要。

多出的运费由谁负担?

从上海到香港的运费由贵方负担。

提单上应该注明"运费预付"字样。

你可以选择宁波作为装运港。

我们希望把上海定为装运港是由于它离货物产地比较近。

II. Role-play

1. Lydia Wang is discussing with Ella Black about the delivery of the products.

Miss Black wants an early delivery and urges an earlier shipment.

Lydia Wang insists on the shipment in October.

2. Lydia Wang is discussing with Ella Black about the delivery of the products.

Miss Black asks whether the shipment could be in the early of October.

Lydia Wang explains that the factories are fully committed.

They agree on a partial shipment.

III. Dubbing

It's time for you to practice your spoken English for international business.

Conversation One

Conversation Two

Conversation Three

Section C
Lessons from the Professionals

Read the following article. There may be *some mistakes* in the use of English as well as in the operation or understanding of foreign trade. Discuss with your classmates and try to find some solutions to the problems concerning international trade.

To the greenhand
alexnee

I'd like to share my experience which i went through in the past 3 years, which I think may bring you help to get orders.

Firstly, you should know your position, you are a greenhand, everyone in your company is your teacher, what they did to you is reasonable, even if it is obviously unfair to you; never imply yourself as a students from XX school.

Secondly, you should have an active and positive manner in the job, especially during in practice period; do what you can do; ask the old colleague directly and politly. Never waiting for the other give you help kindly.

Thirdly, you should know the product very well in the practice period, the bottom line is that you can match the model with the product as well as the details, such as packing, structure, the new design, the certificates and things like that. Never thinking you wanna make big deals in the first months, just do your homework at the first step.

Fourth. To be sure get alone with your new colleague as well as keep yourself in an indepedent situation, i understand it seems inconsistent, but it is a lesson you have to learn to deal with, especailly you are working for a big company.

Task Eleven Payment Negotiation

任务十一 谈判与磋商——支付方式

Learning Objective

Be aware of the advantages and disadvantages of payment by L/C.
Be able to enquire, explain and refuse payment terms during negotiation.

My Gains

Business etiquette	
Work skills	
Language skills	

My Problems

Business etiquette	
Work skills	
Language skills	

Section A
Movie Time

Watch the video clip and answer the question.

What happens in the negotiation? If you were there, what negotiating tactic would you adopt?

The Apprentice: The Price Is Height

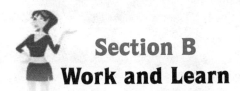

Section B
Work and Learn

usiness Communication Skills

The Importance of Business Communication

Effective communication is all about conveying your messages to other people clearly and unambiguously. It's also about receiving information that others are sending to you, with as little distortion as possible.

Doing this involves effort from both the sender of the message and the receiver. In fact, communication is only successful when both the sender and the receiver understand the same information as a result of the communication.

Being able to communicate effectively is therefore essential if you want to build a successful career. Regardless of the size of business you are in — whether a large corporation, a small company, or even a home-based business — effective communication skills are essential for success.

ork Skills—Improving Negotiation Skills (3)

① During the negotiation process, what can you do to produce a mutually beneficial outcome?

② What do you know about payment and payment terms?

Words and Expressions

- ✓ Letter of Credit (L/C)
- ✓ form of credit
- ✓ validity
- ✓ expiry date
- ✓ date of issue
- ✓ L/C amount
- ✓ to open by airmail
- ✓ to open by cable
- ✓ Telegraphic Transfer (T/T)
- ✓ Demand Draft (D/D)
- ✓ Mail Transfer (M/T)
- ✓ Cash on Delivery (COD) / Pay on Delivery (POD)
- ✓ Cash with Order (CWO)
- ✓ Cash against Document (CAD)
- ✓ Clean Bill for Collection
- ✓ Documentary Bill for Collection
- ✓ irrevocable L/C
- ✓ confirmed L/C
- ✓ unconfirmed L/C
- ✓ Documents against Payment (D/P)
- ✓ Documents against Payment at Sight
- ✓ Documents against Payment after Sight
- ✓ Documents against Acceptance (D/A)

Useful Sentence Patterns

- ✓ What is your proposition on terms of payment?
- ✓ What is your regular practice about terms of payment?
- ✓ How are we going to arrange payment?
- ✓ Shall we discuss the mode of payment?
- ✓ Now let's discuss the question of payment terms.
- ✓ Talk about terms of payment, could you advise me of your regular practice in this respect?
- ✓ Will you make your payment terms easier for us?
- ✓ Could you tell me which kind of payment terms you'll choose?
- ✓ What do you think of the payment terms?
- ✓ Your offer is attractive, but we require payment by L/C.
- ✓ Invoice would be payable within thirty days of receipt.

✓ Payment by L/C is our usual practice.

✓ As a general rule, the expiry date of the L/C is to be 15 days after the shipment date, leaving enough time for negotiation.

✓ The L/C shall remain valid until the 14th day after the shipment.

✓ We are not familiar with your opening bank, so we require the L/C be confirmed by a bank acceptable to us.

✓ We refer you to The Bank of Switzerland if you wish to make any inquiries on our credit standing.

✓ Our terms of payment are by irrevocable L/C payable by sight draft against presentation of shipping documents.

✓ We regret we can't accept payment "cash against document."

✓ We'll agree to change the terms of payment from L/C at sight to D/P at sight.

✓ We can do the business on 60 days D/P basis.

✓ We'll draw D/P against your purchase.

✓ We can't agree to draw at 30 days D/A.

✓ It would help me greatly if you would accept D/A or D/P.

✓ Could you make an exception and accept D/A or D/P?

✓ Can you tell it on an installment basis?

✓ Do you accept payment by installments?

✓ We can't accept D/P or D/A. We insist on payment by L/C.

✓ What is the period of validity of this L/C?

 ample Dialogue

Tuesday, June 8, 2010
Ding Na and Eddie Collins are negotiating about terms of payment.

D: We've settled the question of price, packing and shipment. Now let's come to the terms of payment.

C: Sure, as an importer, we insist on payment in cash on delivery.

D: Sorry, we won't accept payment in cash on delivery. As a rule, we don't accept other payment terms except L/C.

C: You know, our company enjoys a good prestige in this line. I don't think it is necessary for you to feel worried about the matter of our credit standing.

D: Yes, I believe it. But I am afraid I can do nothing about it. L/C will be good to both of us. Since this is our first deal, it will be better to insist on L/C payment terms.

C: That is true, but to speak frankly, to open L/C is really troublesome and costs us a lot. Miss Ding, I still wonder if you could make an exception and accept D/A for this order?

D: We can't accept D/A, but we may make an exception to accept D/P.

C: Then, could you accept payment by D/P at 30 days sight?

D: If so, there will be no great difference. We only accept D/P at sight.

C: Oh, I see.

D: You should make payment against our documentary draft upon presentation. The shipping documents are to be delivered to you against payment only.

C: All right. Hope everything will be fine.

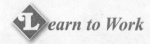

earn to Work

I. Try them in English

1. Words and Expressions

信用证

到期日

信开

电开

电汇

票汇

信汇

不可撤消的信用证

付款交单

承兑交单

2. Sentences

你们通常采用什么样的付款条件？

我们怎样确定付款条件呢？

我们来谈谈付款方式好吗？

你们采取什么付款方式？

能否告知你们将采用哪种付款方式？

对支付条件有何看法？

你方价格很有吸引力，但是我们要求用信用证支付。

我们的付款条件是保兑的不可撤消的以买方为受益人的信用证。

收到发票后30天内付款。

信用证直至装运后第十四天均有效。

我们不熟悉贵公司的开证行，所以我们要求该证由一家我们认可的银行保兑。

如对本公司信用状况有任何疑问，请向瑞士银行查询。

很抱歉，我们不能接受凭单付款办法。

我们同意将即期信用证付款方式改为即期付款交单。

我们可以按60天付款交单的方式进行交易。

您能否来个例外，接受D/A或D/P付款方式？

你们这里可以分期付款吗？

你同意分期付款吗？

II. Role-play

 Lydia Wang and Ella Black are negotiating about the terms of payment.

Lydia Wang suggests payment by L/C.

Ella Black wants to pay by installment.

 Lydia Wang and Ella Black are negotiating about the terms of payment.

Lydia Wang suggests a payment by L/C.

Ella Black wants to pay by T/T or D/P.

Ella Black makes a concession by offering a 50% by L/C and the balance by D/P.

Lydia Wang sticks to the payment by L/C.

III. Dubbing

It's time for you to practice your spoken English for international business.

Conversation One

Conversation Two

Conversation Three

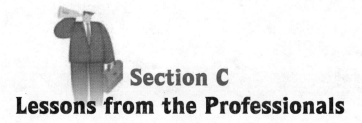

Section C
Lessons from the Professionals

Read the following article. There may be *some mistakes* in the use of English as well as in the operation or understanding of foreign trade. Discuss with your classmates and try to find some solutions to the problems concerning international trade.

how to contact the old customer

Tonilzx

I have the cusotmer's contact information but i don't know how about contact them . Who could let us know about it? some of them you have contacted as before and quote the price but without the business together? How to keep in touch with them will be better?

lily_trade

I contact them when we have new products come out~

Some festivals are good chance as well~

bebe11

If you have never had a contact w/ these old customers, then you can send them a email to introduce yourself to them, and let them know to contact you directly if they have any inquiries. You got their contact info from your companys' record, and you have no contact to each other for quite a while. Now, you just want to say "Hi" and want to keep in touch w/ them...

Your company just launch a new product and would like to introduce to them... A special promotion or discount... just try to think of any excuse to send them email, i hope the above ideas are useful to you.

zqqd1983

In fact, it is not a difficult thing to contact with the previous customer, the key point is how to start the communication between us. Once we have a good start, it will be easy for us to go on our talking.

The suggestion is that you can send them when you have lauched the good products, or say best wishes when holiday, or you can say a simple sentence, such as "long time have no chatting", "how are you these days" and so on. All in all,the aim is let them know you are still existed, and not forget you, then maybe when they are intent to purchase, it is possible for them to inquire you.

Task Twelve Contract

任务十二 签订合同

Learning Objective

Be aware of the basic knowledge of business contract.
Be able to express your ideas about the contract terms.
Be able to talk with the client about signing the contract.

My Gains

Business etiquette	
Work skills	
Language skills	

My Problems

Business etiquette	
Work skills	
Language skills	

Section A
Movie Time

Watch the video clip and answer the question.

How would Edward know that McNeil will refuse to make further concession?

Starting Business English: Negotiating Prices (2)

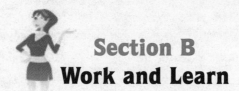

Section B
Work and Learn

usiness Communication Skills

Customer Service Skills May Give Businesses Competitive Edge

Find simple ways to offer excellent customer service in order to foster customer satisfaction and loyal clientele which may increase profits. When one is transmitting information internally, one's tone tends to be friendlier and rather informal, but when one is transmitting information externally, one's tone tends to be more reserved and formal. On the other hand, there are different levels of internal communication: for example, when an employee is conversing with a coworker, he or she is likely to use different wording, phrasing, inflection and intonation than when conversing with a supervisor or the company's president.

The Challenge of External Communication

Communicating externally is far more challenging than communicating internally, mainly because when members are communicating with people outside the organization, not only are they representing themselves as individuals, but also the organization as a whole.

Subsequently, whenever members place a telephone call; send an advertisement, business letter, or e-mail; or conduct a face-to-face meeting on the organization's behalf, these members are making an impression that can possibly mean either success or failure for the organization.

ork Skills—Signing the Contract

1 What are the basic elements needed to create a valid business contract?

2 What will a contract cover?

3 What are the rules for the writing of a business contract?

ords and Expressions

- ✓ sign a contract
- ✓ originals of the contract
- ✓ one month notice
- ✓ unanimous
- ✓ comment
- ✓ clause
- ✓ terms
- ✓ stipulation
- ✓ penalty
- ✓ arbitration
- ✓ revise
- ✓ cancel
- ✓ be entitled to
- ✓ come into force

seful Sentence Patterns

- ✓ Do you mean there's something you are not clear about?
- ✓ I need to know more about…
- ✓ I respect your decision.
- ✓ We both want to sign a contract, and we have to make some concessions to do it.
- ✓ These are two originals of the contract we prepared.
- ✓ This is our contract. Please read it carefully before signing.
- ✓ We enclose our sales contract No.45 in duplicate.
- ✓ May I refer you to the contract stipulation about packing (or shipping)?
- ✓ The contract states that the supplier will be charged a penalty if there is a delay in delivery.
- ✓ We have reached an agreement on all the terms. So there shouldn't be any problem for the contract.
- ✓ May we once more remind you that the contract should be cancelled by one month notice.
- ✓ We always carry out the terms of our contract to the letter and stand by what we say.

✓ In case one party fails to carry out the contract, the other party is entitled to cancel the contract.

✓ This contract will come into force as soon as it is signed by two parties.

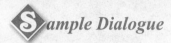 **S**ample Dialogue

Tuesday, June 8, 2010

Everything goes smoothly. Ding Na and Eddie Collins are going to sign the contract.

C: Miss Ding, I made a very close study of the draft contract.

D: Any questions?

C: Yes. There are a few points which I'd like to bring up. First, the packing stipulated in the contract should be clearly written as inner packing and outer packing. The exporter will follow the packing instruction of the importer.

D: I see.

C: Second, about the terms of payment. Your draft contract says that payment is to be made by L/C, while we've exchange our opinion that we'll pay by D/P at sight. Is that right?

D: I will check it later.

C: And the third point is about arbitration. It's stipulated that arbitration shall take place in China. In all our past contracts signed with other suppliers, it was stipulated that arbitration took place in a third country.

D: Yes, that's right.

C: But how is it that you wish to have it carried out in China?

D: Shall we take up the matter point by point?

C: That's a good idea.

D: Now, the first point is about packing. We agree to write the details about packing in the contract. It will be convenient for both of us. And we'd also like to add "One copy of the packing instruction required" into the contract when you present the document.

C: This can easily be done.

D: Second, about terms of payment by L/C, we will change it to D/P at sight.

C: Thank you.

D: As for arbitration, in our dealings with many countries, arbitration is to be carried out in China. China International Economic and Trade Arbitration Commission enjoys a high prestige among friendly companies. Personally I hope you'll accept this clause. Further more, the disputes that arose from our business transaction were all settled through friendly consultations. Very rarely was arbitration resorted to.

C: I see. The new arbitration clause is acceptable.

D: Is there anything else?

C: As far as the contract stipulations are concerned, there is nothing more. Thank you very much. When should we sign the contract?

D: We'll revise the contract and have it ready to be signed this afternoon at half past three. How's that?

C: Perfect.

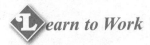

I. Try them in English

1. Words and Expressions

签订合同

合同正本

（解约前）一个月后离职通知

全体一致的；无异议的

评论，意见

（法律文件等的）条款

条件，条款

契约；规定

罚款

仲裁

修改

废除，取消

有……的资格；有权

开始生效

2. Sentences

你是说有不清楚的地方？

我需要多知道些有关……的情况。

我尊重你的意见。

我们都想签合同，因此双方都要做些让步。

这是我们准备好的两份合同正本。

这是我们的合同。请仔细阅读后再签字。

附上我们第45号销售合同一式两份。

请您看看合同中有关包装（装运）的规定。

合同规定如果供货商延误交货期，将被罚款。

我们对各项条款意见都一致了。合同应当没什么问题了。

请允许我们再次提醒您，双方应在取消合同一个月前进行通知。

我们坚持重合同，守信用。

如果一方不执行合同，另一方有权撤消该合同。

合同一经双方签订即生效。

II. Role-play

1️⃣ Lydia Wang and Ella Black have concluded the deal and getting ready for signing the contract. They go over the terms in the contract.

2️⃣ Lydia Wang and Ella Black are getting ready for signing the contract. They go over the terms in the contract. They hold a discussion over the destination port, mode of transport and other terms.

III. Dubbing

It's time for you to practice your spoken English for international business.

Conversation One

Conversation Two

Conversation Three

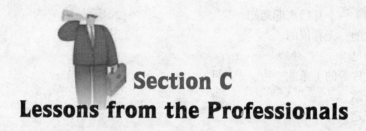

Section C
Lessons from the Professionals

Read the following article. There may be *some mistakes* in the use of English as well as in the operation or understanding of foreign trade. Discuss with your classmates and try to find some solutions to the problems concerning international trade.

My talk to a customer

Mypenny

I sent our price lists to one customer, and after waiting for several days, I meet her on SKYPE and asked her: "How are you? Don't forget me, hah. What do you think of our price?" But my customer didn't reply me.

suline

These things I see many, when we are one of the member of the alibaba, I always quote but receive nothing. Maybe many clients just want to know the price about the products, maybe they do not need these products, maybe they will need them later. who knows.

solso2008

perhaps he is very busy, and he is tired of your quotation, he is not intested in your price.

Karolina

hehe...that's normal, i met many customers like that. But never give up, keep trying, may you success!

sherry qian268

I think I could give you some reply, As a member of importer, everyday I get too many spam mails or messgages, you know some salesman have not check the customer requirements and send too long introduction about their company and products, even same mail sent for many times, \Now I just see the title and then delete the these mails directly, in other words, most of china mails are spam mails. Sines

chorly

It is normal, they were receiving most quotation from so many companies, maybe they are busy, you can try to persuade your good products of good service, maybe next time he will turn to you again.

Task Thirteen Business Dinner

任务十三 商务宴请

Learning Objective

Be aware of some intercultural communication skills: basic table manners.
Be able to host a business dinner.

My Gains

Business etiquette	
Work skills	
Language skills	

My Problems

Business etiquette	
Work skills	
Language skills	

Section A
Movie Time

Watch the video clip and answer the question.

What are the major duties of the two assistants in this benefit?

The Devil Wears Prada

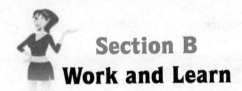

Section B
Work and Learn

Business Communication Skills

How to Use Your Body Language (1)

There is no specific advice on how to use your body language. What you do might be interpreted in several ways, depending on the setting and who you are talking to. You'll probably want to use your body language differently when talking to your boss compared to when you talk to a girl/guy you're interested in. These are some common interpretations of body language and often more effective ways to communicate with your body.

First, to change your body language. You must be aware of your body language. Notice how you sit, how you stand, how you use you hands and legs, what you do while talking to someone.

You might want to practice in front of a mirror. Yeah, it might seem silly but no one is watching you. This will give you good feedback on how you look to other people and give you an opportunity to practice a bit before going out into the world.

Another tip is to close your eyes and visualize how you would stand and sit to feel confident, open and relaxed or whatever you want to communicate. See yourself move like that version of yourself. Then try it out.

You might also want to observe friends, role models, movie stars or other people you think has good body language. Observe what they do and you don't. Take bits and pieces you like from different people. Try using what you can learn from them.

Some of these tips might seem like you are faking something. But fake it till you make it a useful way to learn something new. And remember, feelings work backwards too. If you smile a bit more you will feel happier. If you sit up straight you will feel more energetic and in control. If you slow down your movements you'll feel calmer. Your feelings will actually reinforce your new behaviours and feelings of weirdness will dissipate.

In the beginning, it's easy to exaggerate your body language. You might sit with your legs almost ridiculously far apart or sit up straight in a tense pose all the time. That's Ok. And people aren't looking as much as you think, they are worrying about their own problems. Just play around a bit, practice and monitor yourself to find a comfortable balance.

Work Skills—Business Meal Etiquette Skills

1 What's the function of business dinners?

2 What do you need to do to make the dinner pleasant and profitable?

Words and Expressions

- ✓ in honor of
- ✓ propose a toast
- ✓ cheers
- ✓ to your success
- ✓ specialty
- ✓ first course / starters
- ✓ main course
- ✓ cold dishes
- ✓ dessert
- ✓ beverage
- ✓ soup
- ✓ Chinese food
- ✓ Sichuan Cuisine

Useful Sentence Patterns

- ✓ How are you making out in Hangzhou?
- ✓ It's a pleasure to have you here.
- ✓ It's very kind of you to have invited me.
- ✓ I'm happy to host this dinner party in honor of our friends.

✓ We are very honored to be invited to this magnificent dinner.

✓ Here is your seat.

✓ Dinner is ready.

✓ It's really delicious.

✓ What beautiful colors.

✓ They look really inviting.

✓ I'd like to try some Chinese food.

✓ Chinese food is divided into eight big cuisines, or say, eight styles, such as Cantonese food, Beijing food, Sichuan food, etc.

✓ Is there any difference between Cantonese food and Beijing food?

✓ Cantonese food is lighter while Beijing food is heavy and spicy. Most Sichuan dishes are spicy and hot.

✓ Are you ready to order?

✓ Excuse me, could I see the menu, please?

✓ So what's your recommendation for me?

✓ Please make yourself at home.

✓ Help yourself please.

✓ What would you like to drink?

✓ To your health and success in business.

✓ I wish to propose a toast to our friendship and cooperation.

✓ Thank you for your hospitality and your dinner.

✓ At this point, I propose a toast to the cooperation between…and… Cheers!

ample Dialogue

Tuesday, June 8, 2010

The negotiation is brought to a successful close. In the evening, Ding Na, together with Lydia Wang, is hosting a dinner party in honor of Mr. Collins at Hangzhou Dahua Hotel. Young Gang, general manager of K&S Group, attends the party and expresses his good wishes for future cooperation.

D: Mr. Collins, it's a pleasure to have you here.

C: It's very kind of you to have invited me.

Y: Good evening, Mr. Collins. On behalf of our corporation, I want to extend our warm welcome to you and to thank you for the cooperation you have shown us.

C: Thank you for your kind words, Mr. Young. You know, we do value our association with K&S Group.

Y: We hope this will be a good start to a long and profitable business relationship.

C: So do I.

Y: Well, Mr. Collins, how are you making out in Hangzhou?

C: Gorgeous. Hangzhou is an amazing city. Flowers everywhere. Miss Ding and Miss Wang are very helpful and kind.

D: It's our great pleasure to work with you.

W: Here is our first dish. Please be seated.

C: What beautiful colours! They look really inviting.

D: Please help yourself, Mr. Collins.

Y: May I propose a toast to the success of our negotiation and our friendship?

All: Cheers!

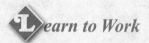

earn to Work

I. Try them in English

1. Words and Expressions

为了向……表示敬意

致祝酒辞；敬酒

干杯

为生意兴隆（干杯）

特制品，特产，名产

第一道菜 / 开胃菜

主菜

冷菜

甜食

饮料

汤

中餐

川菜

2. Sentences

在杭州过得怎么样？

欢迎光临。

非常感谢您的盛情邀请。

非常高兴能为朋友举办这次晚宴。

我们非常荣幸能被邀请参加这个盛宴。

请入席！

饭菜已经准备好了。

味道真的好极了。

色彩太漂亮了。

它们看起来真诱人。

我想尝尝中国菜。

中国菜分成八大菜系，或者说八种风味。如广东菜、北京菜、四川菜等等。

广东菜和北京菜有什么不同吗？

广东菜清淡适口，而北京菜则味重香浓，四川菜大都麻辣浓香。

您现在可以点餐吗？

打扰一下，我能看看菜单吗？

那么你给我推荐几道菜吧。

请不要客气！

请各位随意用餐。

您喝点什么？

为你的身体健康、生意兴隆干杯。

我提议为我们的友谊和合作干杯。

感谢你们的盛情和晚宴。

现在我提议，为了……和……之间的合作干杯！

II. Role-play

Lydia Wang invites Eddie Collins out for lunch.

Mr. Collins wants to go to a Chinese restaurant.

Lydia recommends Sichuan food.

Mr. Collins wishes to try Dongpo Pork.

Lydia Wang and Mr. Collins enter a newly opened restaurant.

They order some dishes.

III. Dubbing

It's time for you to practice your spoken English for international business.

Conversation One

Conversation Two

Conversation Three

Section C
Lessons from the Professionals

Read the following article. There may be *some mistakes* **in the use of English as well as in the operation or understanding of foreign trade. Discuss with your classmates and try to find some solutions to the problems concerning international trade.**

Funny experience

lily_trade

Every time when I eating with customers outside at restaurant, there will always have one interesting image in my mind.

I still remember clearly that was one year ago, there were three customers which is from one family, father, mother & son, all of these three are kind & optimistic, after long times' negotiation about business, it was time for supper, so I decided to bring them to a Western-style restaurant which they like beefsteak very much.

They all asked me to recommend the steaks to them, they said they believe my recommendation. Well, that was really a big task to me, anway, i just accepted the suggestions from the waiters & finally the food have confirmed. But the worst matter was about condiments towards the steak which the menu didnt show those clearly in English!! When waiters asked me which kind of condiments they wanted, I don't know how to say. At that time, I did think those three customers were the kindest ppl I've never met before, they said every condiments are ok for them.

But there was one thing, the son said to me that his mom don't like "spice". God knows that i have throwed most of the English words to my teacher but only a little in my mind now, ya, that means I didnt know what's the meaning of "spice", although the son just explained by gestures with facial expressions. He was very happy after I said I have got his meaning, but only God knew how confused I was at that time, but I just told to waiter that his mom didn't need "pepper" on her steak which was bad for her throat, I told them I have got their meaning which I got nothing actually. The mom is really a kind people, although it was not the one she wanted maybe, she told me that: "Lily, wonderful, the steak is very delicious!" Also the son & the father all smiled to me and said yes.

After said goodbye to them & went back to the company, I just checked through the net, I finally got that "spice" is absolutely different with "pepper" Until now I still don't know how did they thought about me when the mum ate the steak without anything left.

Maybe it is not a good history for me, also it is not funny in some distance, after that, I just tried to memorized more words about foods, so I got something from that matter.

I don't know why when asked about the most interssting & hard-forgetted things during my working time, this one will always in my mind, maybe cuz of the son's funny facial expressions & gestures.

Task Fourteen Sightseeing

任务十四 观光游览

Learning Objective

Have a good knowledge of the tourist resources in your city.
Be able to entertain your clients with a pleasant trip to the famous sights of your city.

My Gains

Business etiquette	
Work skills	
Language skills	

My Problems

Business etiquette	
Work skills	
Language skills	

Section A
Movie Time

Watch the video clip and answer the question.

What does the inscription mean?

Roman Holiday

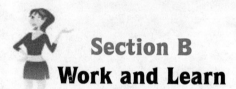

Section B
Work and Learn

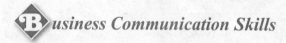

Business Communication Skills

How to Use Your Body Language (2)

1. Don't cross your arms or legs — You have probably already heard you shouldn't cross your arms as it might make you seem defensive or guarded. This goes for your legs too. Keep your arms and legs open.

2. Have eye contact, but don't stare — If there are several people you are talking to, give them all some eye contact to create a better connection and see if they are listening. Keeping too much eye-contact might creep people out. Giving no eye-contact might make you seem insecure.

3. Don't be afraid to take up some space — Taking up space by, for example, sitting or standing with your legs apart a bit signals self-confidence and that you are comfortable in your own skin.

4. Relax your shoulders — When you feel tense it easily winds up as tension in your shoulders. They might move up and forward a bit. Try to relax. Try to loosen up by shaking the shoulders a bit and move them back slightly.

5. Nod when they are talking — nod once in a while to signal that you are listening. But don't overdo it and peck like Woody Woodpecker.

6. Don't slouch, sit up straight — but in a relaxed way, not in a too tense manner.

7. Lean, but not too much — If you want to show that you are interested in what someone is saying, lean toward the person talking. If you want to show that you're confident in yourself and relaxed, lean back a bit. But don't lean in too much or you might seem needy and desperate for some approval. Lean back too much, you might seem arrogant and distant.

8. Smile and laugh — lighten up, don't take yourself too seriously. Relax a bit, smile and laugh when someone says something funny. Smile when you are introduced to someone but don't keep a smile plastered on your face, you'll seem insincere.

9. Don't touch your face — it might make you seem nervous and can be distracting for the listeners or the people in the conversation.

10. Keep your head up — Don't keep your eyes on the ground, it might make you seem insecure and a bit lost. Keep your head up straight and your eyes towards the horizon.

Work Skills—Entertain Clients

1 What is the first thing you need to do to entertain your clients successfully?
2 What are the ways to make conversations with a client interesting?

Words and Expressions

✓ sightseeing
✓ scenic spot
✓ historical relics
✓ tour
✓ start out
✓ join
✓ break
✓ legend
✓ holiday resort
✓ guidebook
✓ itinerary
✓ cruise
✓ colourful
✓ fine and sunny
✓ a full-day tour
✓ exactly my thought

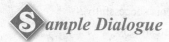seful Sentence Patterns

✓ Does the tour include the zoo?

✓ Where is this tour going?

✓ How long does the tour take?

✓ It's perfect for a cruise.

✓ Please tell me about some interesting places in this city.

✓ Is there anything to visit here?

✓ What are your interests?

✓ What kind of things are you interested in?

✓ I'm interested in architecture.

✓ What kind of tours do you have?

✓ What kind of tours are available?

✓ Would it be all right if I took a picture here?

Sample Dialogue

Wednesday, June 9, 2010

Ding Na takes Eddie Collins on a full-day tour around the West Lake. Mr. Collins suggests going by bike. They ride to the famous sight, Three Pools Mirroring the Moon.

D: Good morning, Mr. Collins. Did you have a good sleep last night?

C: Yes, I had a sound sleep. I feel myself fully recovered.

D: I'm glad to hear that. Can I take you on a one-day tour to some of the scenic spots around the West Lake?

C: Great! I can't wait for that, Miss Ding. It's fine and sunny. Shall we go by bike? I hear we can get a public bike just outside the hotel.

D: Yes, let's go.

(On the way)

D: What do you think of Hangzhou?

C: Hangzhou is an amazing city. The scenery of the West Lake is very charming.

D: Yes, the West Lake is the famous scenic spot in China.

C: "Up above the sky there is a paradise, down on the Earth there are Suzhou and Hangzhou." It really lives up to its reputation.

D: Wow, you are well-informed!

C: I also know ancient people compared the West Lake to a beauty.

D: Yeah. Libai compared the West Lake to a beauty called Xishi in his poem. And now there are 20 scenes in the West Lake, each of them has its own beauty.

C: Yes. Look! The view from here is magnificent.

D: Let me take a picture for you, will you?

C: Yes, please. How's this pose?

D: Um! I'll count to three and click! Smile. One, two, three, okay. Terrific!

C: Thank you, Ding. Oh, look, what are those three stone towers?

D: They are the famous "Three Pools Mirroring the Moon." The three stone miniature pagodas standing in the lake off the isle are presumably the best place for moon viewing. These pagodas produce many magic views of the moon in the water. The stone pagodas are two meters high and each with five equally spaced windows. On the night of the Mid-Autumn Festival, lanterns are put inside the windows. Their lights shine and water near the pagoda reflects the shiny lights and the moon.

C: Wow, it must be a lovely view. I'd like to come back tonight.

 *earn to Work*

I. Try them in English

1. Words and Expressions

观光

景点

古迹

旅行

出发

参加

中断

传说，传奇故事

度假区

旅游指南

旅程；行程（表）

乘船巡游；乘船游览

五彩缤纷

天气晴朗

一日游

正合我意

2. Sentences

这条线路去动物园吗？

这条线路去哪里？

这条线路有多长？

非常适合于乘船游览。

能告诉我这座城市有哪些好玩的地方吗？

这儿有没有可看的地方？

您对什么感兴趣？

我对建筑感兴趣。

都有哪些路线的旅行呢？

您能给我们照张相吗？

II. Role-play

1 Ding Na is talking with Eddie Collins about their plan for a day tour.

Ding Na recommends a tour to Wuzhen.

Mr. Collins is interested in the zoo.

They agree to go to Hangzhou Safari Park.

2 Ella Black is climbing the Great Wall. Lydia Wang is guiding the tour.

III. Dubbing

It's time for you to practice your spoken English for international business.

Conversation One

Conversation Two

Conversation Three

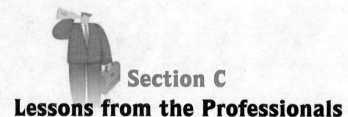

Section C
Lessons from the Professionals

Read the following article. There may be *some mistakes* **in the use of English as well as in the operation or understanding of foreign trade. Discuss with your classmates and try to find some solutions to the problems concerning international trade.**

To get the first order

<u>alexnee</u>

You should learn the saying in your heart: No pain, no gain. Never lose your patience and courage after each fail, remember it is mother of your first order, what you must do is to find out where is the problem, was it because you price you quoted is too high, or the product you offered is not what the clients are looking for. FOB Business Forum is the largest exporter based online community.

Of course, you also need plateform, maybe you register some free members in B2B such as made-in-china, Alibaba, but personally, i think you should get enough luck if you you wanna get order from them. My point is that you should do your best to get chance to the pro. fair and show, it is usually the first step of your successful. If chance coming, you should go to your boss to show him that you are able to do a good a job now, I believe you will get a chance sooner or later. At least, your boss will give you some old clients information.

Now you have some client information, some may from the show/fair, some may from the old client information, some may from B2B; if you are lucky, you may have some inquriies. Anyway, we say the job is on hand.

Follow is my personal idea how to start with the job.

1. Never send all our your product information to your clients, it only means to delect without a look or cheat as span e-mail.

2. collect enough as much information as you can,such as what kind of client company, big or small, what kind of products in there management,what is the style, the basic one or advanced one.

3. Search out the products which may meet your client interest, and never forget to write on your advantages in the mails.

4. Never worried to ask your boss for the best price you can offer, he will think of that you are a hard working employee. who will hate hard-working emplyee? Anyway, Price is the most important point for you to get the order order, cheaper price, more chance. Of course, you should not offer the bottom price at the first time, clients usually like to have a bargain with you, however, cheaper price always means more positive reply.

5. Do the details. I mean we should take care every small details, which makes the clients believe you are a trusted man. I take e-mail for an example, pls make sure nice font, easy and clear words, of course, courtnesy is very important.order doesnot come if you did above, i think you need time, pls never lose heart, order will come sooner or later. business.

Task Fifteen Seeing-off

任务十五 机场送行

Learning Objective

Be aware of some business etiquette of seeing off.
Be able to express your thanks and willingness for future cooperation.

My Gains

Business etiquette	
Work skills	
Language skills	

My Problems

Business etiquette	
Work skills	
Language skills	

Section A
Movie Time

Watch the video clip and answer the question.

Why does the little girl wander away from her mother at the airport?

Flightplan

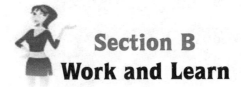

Section B
Work and Learn

***B**usiness Communication Skills*

How to Use Your Body Language (3)

11. Slow down a bit — this goes for many things. Walking slower not only makes you seem more calm and confident, it will also make you feel less stressed. If someone addresses you, don't snap your neck in their direction, turn it a bit more slowly instead.

12. Don't fidget — try to avoid, phase out or transform fidgety movement and nervous ticks such as shaking your leg or tapping your fingers against the table rapidly. You'll seem nervous and fidgeting can be distracting when you try to get something across. Declutter your movements if you are all over the place. Try to relax, slow down and focus your movements.

13. Use your hands more confidently — instead of fidgeting with your hands and scratching your face, use them to communicate what you are trying to say. Use your hands to describe something or to add weight to a point you are trying to make. But don't use them too much or it might become distracting. And don't let your hands flail around, use them with some control.

14. Lower your drink — don't hold your drink in front of your chest. In fact, don't hold anything in front of your heart as it will make you seem guarded and distant. Lower it and hold it beside your leg instead.

15. Realise where your spine ends — many people might sit or stand with a straight back in a good posture. However, they might think that the spine ends where the neck begins and therefore crane the neck forward in a Montgomery Burns-pose. Your spine ends in the back of your head. Keep your whole spine straight and aligned for better posture.

16. Don't stand too close — one of the things we learned from Seinfeld is that everybody gets weirder out by a close-talker. Let people have their personal space, don't invade it.

17. Mirror — often when you get along with a person, when the two of you get a good connection, you will start to mirror each other unconsciously. That means that you mirror the other person's body language a bit. To make the connection better you can try a bit of proactive mirroring. If he leans forward, you might lean forward. If she holds her hands on her thighs, you might do the same. But don't react instantly and don't mirror every change in body language. Then weirdness will ensue.

18. Keep a good attitude — last but not least, keep a positive, open and relaxed attitude. How you feel will come through in your body language and can make a major difference.

ork Skills—Seeing-off and Gift-giving

1 What do you know about the etiquette concerning seeing-off?
2 Is it a MUST to give a gift to your client?

ords and Expressions

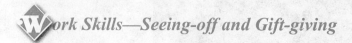

- ✓ superior
- ✓ see sb. off
- ✓ airport
- ✓ passport
- ✓ the Inspection Post
- ✓ customs
- ✓ promote
- ✓ souvenir
- ✓ gift
- ✓ token

seful Sentence Patterns

- ✓ It's a rewarding trip!
- ✓ How time flies! / Time really passes quickly. / Time is flying.
- ✓ I must say goodbye to you.
- ✓ Well, I'd better be on my way.
- ✓ I'm sorry, but I've got to be on my way.

✓ I think it's about time we got going.

✓ I really have to rush.

✓ Thank you so much for coming.

✓ Hope you'll come again.

✓ Hope you'll visit Hangzhou again.

✓ We'll be sorry to see you leave so soon.

✓ It's a shame that you have to leave./ It's a pity you are leaving so soon.

✓ I hope you've enjoyed your stay in China.

✓ I appreciate what you have done for me very much. Everything I have seen here has left a deep impression on me.

✓ I'm sure your visit will help to promote the friendship and understanding between both of us.

✓ Please accept this as a souvenir for our friendship.

✓ This little gift is a token of our regard.

✓ Thank you very much for coming all the way to see me off.

✓ Thank you for your hospitality and thoughtful arrangement.

✓ I enjoyed myself very much.

✓ What time will we be boarding?

✓ It's time to board the plane.

✓ Good-bye and happy landing!

✓ Have a splendid voyage.

✓ May you have a fine trip!

✓ Have a pleasant trip!

✓ A pleasant journey to you!

✓ A pleasant journey.

✓ Hope you have a smooth trip.

✓ Bon voyage!

✓ Safe flight.

 *ample Dialogue*

Thursday, June 10, 2010
Eddie Collins is leaving for Beijing.
Ding Na is at Hangzhou International Airport again.
She is seeing him off.

D: Here we are.

C: Oh, the queue is very long.

D: You can check in at Business Class over there.

C: Oh, of course. Thank you.

Clerk: Hello, how are you? Could I see your ticket and passport, please?

C: Here you are.

Clerk: Thank you. How many pieces of luggage?

C: Four.

Clerk: Place them on the scales please. This one could go on as carry-on luggage if you like.

C: No, it's fine. Thanks.

Clerk: Here is your boarding pass. Your flight will be boarding at Gate 15 from 12:10. Please pass through security no later than 11:30. Enjoy your trip.

C: Thank you. Well, it's time to go now, Miss Ding.

D: Sorry to see you leave. We'd like you to accept this little present as a souvenir of China.

C: Well, what a lovely gift! Thank you very much!

D: I'm glad you like it. I hope you've enjoyed your stay in Hangzhou.

C: Of course, I appreciate what you have done for me very much. I won't forget my days here.

D: It's been lovely working with you. I'm sure your visit will help to promote the friendship and cooperation between both of us.

C: Same here. And if you are ever in our neck of the woods, please look us up.

D: Thank you. I'll remember that. And I believe we'll have further contact in the future. Safe flight.

C: Goodbye.

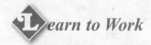earn to Work

I. Try them in English

1. Words and Expressions

（品质、程度）优良的；较好的

送行，送别

机场

护照

检查站

进口税；海关

促进，推动，提升

纪念品

礼物

象征；代币

2. Sentences

不虚此行！

时间过得真快！

我必须要和你告别了。

好啦，我该走了。

很抱歉我必须走了。

我想差不多是告辞的时候了。

我真的得赶快走了。

感谢光临！

欢迎再来！

欢迎以后再来杭州！

真遗憾您这么快就要走了。

真遗憾您要走了。

希望您在中国度过的时光是快乐的。

十分感谢您对我的关照，在中国见到的一切给我留下了深刻的印象。

我坚信您的来访将促进我们双方的友谊和了解。

请接受这个作为我们友谊的纪念品。

这点礼物是我们的一点心意。

非常感谢您老远来为我送行。

谢谢您的热情接待和周到安排。

我玩得非常开心尽兴。

请问我们什么时间登机？

该登机了。

再见，一路顺风！

II. Role-play

 Lydia Wang is at the airport.

Ella Black is going back to America.

Lydia Wang is seeing her off.

They exchange gifts.

 Lydia Wang is at the airport.

Ella Black is going back to America.

Lydia Wang is seeing her off.

She helps Ella with the check-in.

She gives her a gift.

They say goodbye to each other.

III. Dubbing

It's time for you to practice your spoken English for international business.

Conversation One

Conversation Two

Conversation Three

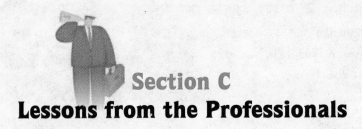

Section C
Lessons from the Professionals

Read the following article. There may be *some mistakes* in the use of English as well as in the operation or understanding of foreign trade. Discuss with your classmates and try to find some solutions to the problems concerning international trade.

一个老外给外贸人的建议

As a sourcing agent and buyer I can tell you what is a good quotation for me: it includes all relevant information! My job is to find a reliable supplier at a reasonable price in the shortest time possible.

It is very possible that I will choose a supplier whose price is a few percent higher but the quotation is complete. That means, it includes: - FOB price, with seaport marked! (I often get FOB quotes without location. Obviously for me in Europe a FOB Shanghai price is higher than a FOB Xiamen price, since shipping rates are different).

— Delivery time (so far no Chinese supplier was able to keep the promised delivery time for my projects — 90% delay, 10% early)

— Package unit (carton details) Carton weight, size, volume, content, material. It is very important. Usually this point is simply left out by suppliers. But I — and most full-time buyers — have just simply no time to beg for any details separately. If a quotation misses this, I simply delete it. I have no time to ask for these points, but I can only calculate my shipping cost with this info.

— Payment conditions must be exactly discussed.

I hope suppliers will consider these points in the future. If you include all relevant information, you can really help your partner in his decision. And for the supplier, it is a job done once, you needn't work out each detail separately.

References

参考书目

[1] 曹菱. 外贸英语实务 [M]. 北京：外语教学与研究出版社，2003.4

[2] 帅建林. 国际贸易实务 [M]. 成都：西南财经大学出版社，2005.3

[3] 凌华倍. 外经贸英语函电与谈判 [M]. 北京：中国对外经济贸易出版社，2002.7

[4] 刘文宇等.《商务英语口语大全》[M]. 大连：大连理工大学出版社，2007.9

[5] 孙耀远等.《商务英语口语365》[M]. 上海：上海教育出版社，2007.9

[6] 浩瀚.《商务英语情景会话模版》[M]. 北京：国防工业出版社，2007.1

[7] 耿小辉等.《英语口语话题王》[M]. 北京：中国科学文化音像出版社，2007.3

[8] 戴卫平等.《英语口语语料库》[M]. 大连：大连理工大学出版社，2006.5

《商务英语口语》

尊敬的老师：

　　您好！

　　为了方便您更好地使用本教材，获得最佳教学效果，我们特向使用该书作为教材的教师赠送本教材配套参考资料，包括经典视频片段、学生MP3、电子版教师用书和教学课件。如有需要，请完整填写"教师联系表"并加盖所在单位系（院）公章，免费向出版社索取。

北京大学出版社

✂ -

教 师 联 系 表

教材名称	《商务英语口语》				
姓名：	性别：		职务：		职称：
E-mail：		联系电话：		邮政编码：	
供职学校：			所在院系：		
					（章）
学校地址：					
教学科目与年级：			班级人数：		
通信地址：					

　　填写完毕后，请将此表邮寄给我们，我们将为您免费寄送本教材配套资料，谢谢！

北京市海淀区成府路205号

北京大学出版社外语编辑部　朱丽娜　　　邮 购 部 电话：010-62534449

邮政编码：　100871　　　　　　　　　市场营销部电话：010-62750672

电子邮箱：zln0120@163.com　　　　　外语编辑部电话：010-62759634